KU-718-108

DANIEL: AN ACTIVE VOLCANO

DANIEL:
AN ACTIVE VOLCANO

Reflections on the Book of Daniel

D S Russell

THE SAINT ANDREW PRESS
· EDINBURGH ·

First published in 1989 by
THE SAINT ANDREW PRESS
121 George Street, Edinburgh, EH2 4YN

Copyright © D S Russell 1989

ISBN 0–7152–0632–X

All rights reserved. No part of this publication may be reproduced or
transmitted in any form or by any means, electronic or mechanical,
including photocopy, recording, or information storage and retrieval
system, without permission in writing from the publisher. This book
is sold subject to the condition that it shall not, by way of trade or
otherwise, be lent, re-sold, hired out or otherwise circulated without
the publisher's prior consent.

All biblical references from RSV unless otherwise stated.

British Library Cataloguing in Publication Data
Russell, D. S. (David Syme), *1916–*
Daniel.
1. Bible. O.T. Daniel
I. Title
224'.5

ISBN 0–7152–0632–X

Typeset by J&L Composition Ltd, 1 Mitford St., Filey, N. Yorks.

Contents

Preface

For many years past I have been interested in the apocalyptic writings of the so-called intertestamental period and have tried to clarify to myself and hopefully to others their significance for the times in which they were produced. At the same time I have tried to discover what relevance their message may have for the days in which we ourselves are now living. Of particular interest in this connection is the Book of Daniel which, it must be said, has suffered much at the hands of those who would find in it secret codes which would unlock the mysteries of the ages and not least confirm the hope that 'the end is nigh'.

In my small commentary on *Daniel*, published in 1981 by The Saint Andrew Press and the Westminster Press in the Daily Study Bible series, I endeavoured to rescue the book from such prognostications and to indicate that, despite its strange symbolic language and its extravagant style, it nevertheless has a message for today which is well worth listening to as a word of God for our time. The more I have read it, the more I have become convinced that this is so.

This present small volume is an attempt to take further what was said in that earlier commentary. Its title echoes some words of the Swiss pastor, Walter Lüthi, in his book, *The Church to Come* (English ed., 1939), written during the threatening years of the 1930s. Daniel is indeed 'molten lava', devastating in its judgment of evil and destructive of tyranny and oppression. I trust that this little volume will help in some way to make its message heard again in our own troubled world.

Bristol, 1988   D S Russell

Introduction

1   Reflections on Daniel

A number of 'critical' commentaries and introductions relating to the Book of Daniel have been long available which give a careful analysis of such matters as date of composition, oral and literary sources, authorship, provenance and so forth. In more recent years several 'theological commentaries' have appeared which, as the name implies, offer a theological interpretation. They point out that Daniel is to be interpreted as sacred scripture, within both Judaism and Christianity, and that in this process of interpretation there is a close relationship between the Old Testament and the New.

The exact nature of that relationship is a matter for ongoing discussion, but for the Christian interpreter of the Old Testament three things at least may be said that are of some significance. *First*, is that there is a need to recognise at all times the integrity of the Old Testament itself as a record of God's dealings with his people Israel and not just as 'a Christian book'. *Second*, is that the Old Testament and the New Testament belong together as a single record of divine revelation, culminating in the life, death and resurrection of Jesus Christ and in the ongoing witness of his Church. *Third*, is that the interpretation of an Old Testament book like that of Daniel is not static but dynamic, showing new insights and understandings in each succeeding generation by the illumination of the Holy Spirit.

This present book does not claim to be a commentary in either the 'critical' or the 'theological' sense of that word, although it will take into serious account the findings of both. It is, as the sub-title indicates, a series of reflections on the text of Daniel in the light of God's revelation in Jesus Christ and in the light also of the world in which we now live. In other words, whilst making use of the findings of modern scholarship, its aim is essentially confessional, homiletical and indeed devotional.

It should not surprise us that, in every succeeding generation, such commentaries and 'reflections' keep on appearing for, although there is a 'once-for-all-ness' about the biblical revelation, there is need to interpret and re-interpret it continually in face of the changing circumstances of the days in which we are living. This being so, it will not suffice to interpret the Old Testament in general, or the Book of Daniel in particular, simply after the manner of, say, the early Church which was of necessity conditioned by its own culture and history and reflected contemporary exegetical traditions, or after the manner of, say, the Reformers who, against their particular historical and religious background, were wont to see in the Old Testament an all-important quarry from which to dig the pure gold of Christian doctrine. It is not to judge either the early Church or the Reformers to say that every age, including our own, must seek to rediscover biblical truth for itself and try to see the meaning of that revelation in terms of the contemporary scene. 'Until the text of the Bible has been shown to be relevant and potent in the immediate social and personal consensus of contemporary life, it has not become the word of God, however faithful the textual exegesis' (*A Kind of Folly*, 1976, p 56). These words of Ian Pitt-Watson, addressed to the preacher, can equally well be addressed to the teacher, the student and the lay person in their reading of the scripture. Reflection and re-interpretation represent an ongoing process, for 'the word of God is living and active' (Heb. 4:12) and continues to speak a vital message for today.

2   Interpreting Daniel as scripture

The indications are that the Book of Daniel came to be recognised as sacred scripture at a fairly early stage in its life due perhaps, in no small measure, to the popular appeal it had during a period of severe testing for the Jewish nation. As such it was subsequently adopted, together with the other scriptures, by the Christian Church which in course of time placed alongside them its own corpus of sacred writings which we know as the New Testament.

In the Hebrew scriptures Daniel is found in the third division of the canon known as *The Writings*, but in the Greek (*Septuagint*) Bible, adopted by the Christian Church, it is placed in the second division called *The Prophets*. Either way it was given a place of honour and recognised as authoritative scripture. It is as such, and not just as a document of value for understanding the history and religion of Judaism at the time when the book was written, that it is the object of study and reflection in this volume.

Although recognised as 'prophetic' within the Christian tradition, Daniel is normally classified as 'apocalyptic', and in this respect corresponds in the Old Testament to the Book of Revelation in the New Testament. It is generally agreed that, whilst prophecy represents the most important source from which apocalyptic grew, there are considerable differences between them, not least in their 'eschatological' expression and understanding. In particular, Daniel makes fairly frequent reference to 'the time of the end' when God's kingdom will appear and the powers of that 'other world' where he dwells with the holy angels will come flooding in. But, as E W Heaton remarks:

> 'the writer was interested not in the mysterious future as such, but in the unveiling of the *present* sovereignty of God. His concern with "the time of the end" was an essentially theological and religious interest, the outcome in a period of intense spiritual agony of his longing for the full manifestation of his conviction that "the Most High ruleth in the kingdom of men"'.
> (*The Book of Daniel*, 1956, p 37).

3 Daniel as 'tract for the times'

Daniel is often referred to as 'a tract for the times' which is of value for the light it casts on the historical events and religious temper of Judaism at the time when the book was written. It is generally agreed that this took place around the year 165 BC in the time of the Seleucid ruler, Antiochus IV (175–63 BC).

The stories contained in chapters 1–6 are told for the most part in the third person; they are popular tales of the exploits of a Jewish exile, Daniel, and his three companions who lived in Babylon in the sixth century where, though restricted in many ways, they did not suffer the kind of persecution which the author's own contemporaries had to endure. These stories no doubt circulated orally for some time before assuming their present form and being joined with the visions around 165 BC. These visions, contained in chapters 7–12, reflect a period of oppression and severe persecution and are for the most part presented in the first person in the name of the Daniel who features in the stories. They thus appear as a pseudonymous writing. On this score, the prophecies contained in these chapters are *vaticinia ex eventu*, prophecies after the event, the second century author being identified with the sixth century hero of the narratives.

These visions, it is to be observed, reflect not some far-distant time when God's kingdom will be ushered in and heaven will replace earth in an age of eternal bliss, but rather the author's own day. The chief enemy is Antiochus IV who, though his exploits are described in symbolic language, is clearly recognisable, as are the other rulers who went before him. Particular attention is paid to his attack on the Jewish religion — he destroys the Torah scrolls, he bans Sabbath observance, he forbids the practice of circumcision, he desecrates the Temple, he erects on the sacred altar an 'abomination' to another god, he commands forbidden animals to be sacrificed, he enforces the eating of swine's flesh, he puts the innocent to the sword. Many apostate Jews sided with him and betrayed the covenant made with their fathers; and many of 'the wise' among the people faced suffering and martyrdom rather than betray their trust. The people are urged to stand firm in the face of such great trial and provocation, to remain true to the covenant made with their fathers and to trust in God that he will indeed deliver them out of the hand of their enemies. The 'end' is coming soon when God will establish his kingdom whose blessings they will share.

It is indeed, then, 'a tract for bad times' which brought much needed comfort and assurance to God's faithful people in one of the most terrible periods in their long history. Interpreted as such, it is a book of considerable worth.

4 Daniel as 'prophetic almanac'

Other interpretations, however, came in course of time to be given to it, as indeed to other books within the 'prophetic canon', which saw in these prophecies a futuristic rather than an historical reference. The prophecy of deliverance made in Daniel referred, it was believed, not to a pending event in the time of the writer, but specifically and indeed solely to the time of the reader. The true meaning of the prophecies was not known even to the one who uttered them in the first place. They had been kept secret and were now being made known for what they truly were and as a clear sign that the end was at hand.

We can imagine the circumstances that led to such a re-interpretation and re-orientation of Daniel's visions. On the death of Antiochus in 163 BC, hopes must have run high that at last the day of deliverance was at hand. But the years passed by and still the kingdom had not come. Could it be that Daniel's prophecies, like that of the fourth kingdom in chapter 7 which would immediately precede the coming of God's kingdom, referred to some world power other than that of Antiochus? Could it be that the reference in that particular prophecy was to the hated Roman empire whose downfall would herald the coming of the kingdom? Such a hope, it is clear, was cherished by the Jews and came to be accepted by the Christians also.

In some such way the prophecies of Daniel were torn from their historical bearings and projected into the future. The way was now open for speculations of all kinds against which the New Testament gives clear warning. Prognostications of 'the end' and calculations concerning the time of its coming were idle pursuits. Such mysteries were known only to God himself and must be left in his hands (*cf* Mark 13:32; Acts 1:7).

These warnings, however, have not always been heeded with the result that, throughout the long centuries, there has been a whole sequence of interpretation and re-interpretation in terms of contemporary or future deliverance. Individuals, nations and events in current history have been recognised as fulfilments of ancient prophecy and as signs that 'the end is at hand'. Dashed hopes have become simply deferred hopes as the scenario has been adapted and new figures substituted for old.

In our own day there has been a strong revival of such hopes and prognostications in the western world (not least in the United States of America) and also in eastern Europe. In the United States it has become big business, particularly through the preaching and teaching of certain influential television evangelists of a fundamentalist persuasion, many of whom would describe themselves as 'premillennial dispensationalists', seeing in this present generation the last of the 'dispensations' into which history is divided and an immediate prelude to the promised kingdom. This kind of expectation of fulfilled prophecy is usually based on such books as Daniel, Ezekiel, the Revelation and other prophetic writings and is closely related to present day politics. It detects in these prophecies exact forecasts concerning countries like the Soviet Union, Red China, the Arab States, the United States of America and Israel, and in so doing illustrates ideological as well as theological presuppositions and predilections on the part of the people concerned. Much of this prognostication is presented in the form of an 'Armageddon theology' which prophesies the inevitability of a great final battle fought with nuclear weapons and leading to the total destruction of the world as a prerequisite of the Second Coming of Christ (see Grace Halsell, *Prophecy and Politics: militant evangelists on the road to nuclear war*, 1986). The danger of such prophecy becoming self-fulfilling is all too apparent, carrying with it a threat to the safety and survival of all mankind.

Interpretation of this kind, with its use of predestinarian prediction, backed up so often by the use of numerology and pseudo-scientific jargon, is surely a complete misuse of scripture. By mechanical manipulation it reduces inspired prophecy to the level of fortune-telling, and divine pronouncement to the level of cosmic horoscope. It is to be rejected because it demonstrates a lack of understanding of the working of God within history as evidenced by scripture and regards the nations and their rulers as mere pawns in a cosmic game in which their fate is determined from the beginning. Its calculation of times and seasons has something in common with post-Daniel apocalyptic thought, but its notion of prediction in terms of precise contemporary fulfilment goes much further and lays itself open to the charge of a speculative subjectivism which it does despite the biblical revelation. The Book of Daniel, when thus used, becomes little more than an *Old Moore's Almanac* in which speculation is substituted for revelation and blind fate for the living God.

5   Daniel as paradigm

But there is yet another approach besides the historical and the futuristic which must claim serious attention. Daniel is to be interpreted as a paradigm, a pattern of God's dealings with men and nations in this and in every age. Such an approach takes seriously the book's historical roots, recognising that it was indeed 'a tract for the times' in which it was written. It takes seriously too its future reference, recognising that prophecy finds fulfilment, not in one particular age only, but in the ongoing purpose of God. The prophecies of Daniel may have found their inspiration and intended fulfilment in the second century BC; but just as clearly they are re-enacted in every society and in every generation in which the forces of light confront the forces of darkness. They declare not a predetermined programme which is to work itself out inexorably and with exact precision in terms of contemporary event, but rather a divine principle which sees God in control of events rather than events in control of God. They assert that Nebuchadnezzar lives today in every proud and arrogant ruler; Daniel and his companions live today in every faithful remnant; and God, who is able to deliver his people from fear as well as from the fiery furnace, also lives today and makes himself known in power to those who put their trust in him.

In this light, prophecies concerning the coming of the kingdom are significant 'not as maps of future history, but as affirmations of the meaning of that history' and of him who is its sovereign Lord. They represent 'an apocalyptic paradigm from which one can conjugate a style of living'. They provide 'a stimulus for the future, not simply a timetable for it'. The eschatological hope they present 'gives energy to (our) evangelical calling' (see W Sibley Towner, 'The Preacher in the

Lions' Den', *Interpreting the Prophets*, J L Mays and P L Achtemeier (eds), 1987, pp 282*f*).

Interpretation of this kind is a judgment of faith. But it is wholly justified, for the Book of Daniel is not simply a Jewish writing put together in 165 BC to reassure the Jewish nation at a time of severe persecution in the reign of Antiochus Epiphanes. It *is* that; but it is at the same time part of sacred scripture whose message can rightly be interpreted within the setting of every age and not least our own. It is at one and the same time an historical document, a future pronouncement and a contemporary record of God's dealings with mankind and his faithfulness shown towards those who readily acknowledge him to be the Lord.

An interesting example of this kind of interpretation in the form of expository preaching is given in Walter Lüthi's book, to which reference has been made in the Preface, which sees the life of Daniel in the sixth century BC reflected clearly in the life of the Confessing Church in Central Europe in the 1930s. Its *modus operandi* is far removed from that of the futurist who prognosticates with precision and confidently identifies current events as the fulfilment of prophecies of long ago. It demonstrates that within this biblical book there are prophetic insights whose relevance extends far beyond the historical situation which gave them birth. In Lüthi's words:

> 'The exposition of the Book of Daniel ... contains a particular message for our time, often in a very startling way ... We are not dealing here with a burnt-out crater. Daniel is AN ACTIVE VOLCANO. Therefore if anyone thinks that it is a matter of playing with cold lava, for edification or otherwise, he should realise that he is playing with fire.'
>
> (*Op. Cit.*, pp ix*f*).

I came to appreciate the significance of these words when I began to write my Daily Study Bible commentary on Daniel which was prepared, not in the scholar's study, but in the midst of inter-Church discussion, human rights debate and interviews with Church and State representatives in East and West Europe. In such circumstances the relevance of Daniel for the Church in this present-day world came home to me with renewed force. This present book is written in the same spirit as a complement and supplement to these earlier reflections. In it I shall try to keep clearly in mind three things: the intention of the writer within the historical situation of the second century BC, the significance of the book as part of the Christian scriptures and the relevance of its stories and visions for the days in which we now live.

These reflections will make plain at least two central truths which remain constant in every generation and find most forceful expression in our own: that faithfulnes to God and obedience to his will may well lead not to prosperity and security, but to suffering and death, and that that will, though impeded for a while, will in the end prevail.

1

In An Alien Land

This opening chapter of the Book of Daniel contains the first of six stories which vividly express the faith of God's people in time of trial. They are followed in later chapters by a series of visions which declare the faithfulness of God and the triumph of his kingdom. Story and vision, different though they may be in their form and in their theological emphases, are brought together to convey a single message in which they complement each other. This complementation is strengthened by reason of the author's adoption of pseudonymity in the second part of the book by which means he writes in the name of the hero of the stories in the first part. Story and vision thus join together to assert that God is in control.

Indeed this fusion of story and vision is characteristic of the Old Testament as a whole. It tells a story which is at the same time a revelation, a story about exodus and exile, showing Yahweh as 'the living God' and demonstrating his divine purpose to redeem and save. It is a story reinforced by vision in which the prophets, for example, see the coming of a new age in which all men will acknowledge his rule over the whole earth. The story and the vision thus belong together in one.

So it is also with the New Testament which complements the Old. It too is a story, a remarkable story, about a man on a mission, about a cross on a hill, about a grave in a garden and about the mighty acts of God made manifest therein. And it is at the same time a vision — a vision of a redeemed humanity and of a new heaven and a new earth. Here again, as in Daniel and in the prophets, story and vision are one, a single vehicle of divine revelation, declaring together both the judgment and the mercy of God.

1   Babylon and Jerusalem

In 597 and again in 587 BC, 'Nebuchadnezzar king of Babylon came to Jerusalem and besieged it' (Dan. 1:1). And, by whatever name, he has been stalking the generations ever since. The first readers of the book, around the year 165 BC, recognised him in their Seleucid overlord Antiochus IV Epiphanes, who, if the truth be told, far outdid his predecessor in cruelty and oppression. Yet other readers in succeeding generations have recognised him in the guise of many more rulers and tyrants, outdoing one another in oppression.

Babylon was the seat of Nebuchadnezzar's empire, a magnificent city with its impressive buildings and hanging gardens and with the glorious temple of the great god Marduk towering over everything else. On each anniversary of the god's coronation hundreds of slaves dragged his huge image through the streets on a great wheeled juggernaut and set it up in his temple in whose vaults lay the sacred vessels pillaged from Jerusalem. Babylon itself was ultimately destroyed and remains today an obscure village in the country of Iraq. But for centuries it has remained a powerful symbol of all that is evil, corrupt and destructive of the truth. To John on the isle of Patmos it represents the Roman empire in the time of Domitian and stands for the forces of evil that seek to crush the young Church (*cf* Rev. 17:5; 18:10,21). To Luther it represents the 'captivity' of the Church to another 'Rome'. But it is much more than this: it represents also, in this and in every age, the captivity of institutions, societies and nations to the forces of materialism, racialism and militarism (to mention only a few) and the captivity of minds and systems to ideologies which capture and enslave.

Jerusalem is the antithesis of Babylon. It is 'the city of peace' whose ramparts protect against the evil forces of darkness, the place where God dwells and where his people dwell with him in safety. The difficulty arises when Babylon is confused with Jerusalem and eventually takes its place, when men call evil good and good evil. To the casual or non-discerning onlooker they may appear very much alike with their great walls, fine buildings and broad streets. One great difference between them is that Babylon seems so much grander, more attractive, more impressive, more invincible. But there is another difference which is more significant still: in Jerusalem there stands, albeit in ruins, the Temple of the living God compared with which the towering temple of Marduk is as a mole-hill. In Jerusalem the Lord God omnipotent reigns.

Babylon will continue to besiege Jerusalem, and again and again will lay it waste. Even the sacred Temple will not be spared. Jeremiah at the time of the exile found that; the writer of Daniel in the time of Antiochus found that; and inmates of the Gulag in our own day have found that. But to all of them the promise is given of restoration, renewal and rebirth. Out of the ruins of the old comes something new and beautiful for God. Even when Jerusalem lies in ruins, Babylon lies under judgment.

2 Exiles in Babylon

'And he brought them to the land of Shinar' (Dan. 1:2). Babylon by any other name is still Babylon. Nebuchadnezzar plundered Jerusalem together with its Temple and carried off its gold plate and bejewelled vessels. But these were only secondary concerns. It was people he was after, not things: 'Then the king commanded Ashpenaz ... to bring some of the people of Israel' (Dan. 1:3). Not just rank-and-file people, but the most able and most influential in the land. Jeremiah, in his prophecy, calls them 'good figs' as distinct from the 'bad figs' who had been left behind (*cf* Jer. 24:1*ff*). Nebuchadnezzar is nothing if not astute.

Among the exiles were Daniel and his three companions who were to demonstrate three things that have brought encouragement and inspiration to the faithful remnant ever since. The first is that God lives in Babylon and not just in Jerusalem. He reigns as king even where Marduk is enthroned. Daniel and his friends no doubt sorely missed the familiar sights and ceremonies in Jerusalem and at first — and perhaps for some considerable time afterwards — must have wondered if their God after all had been left behind. They had been taught that Jerusalem with its Temple was the only place where worship could be offered and sacrifices made, for that was where God dwelt (*cf* Deut. 12:14). Perhaps they recalled how Naaman the leper had taken back to his native land 'two mules' burden of earth' from Israel so that he could somehow still have some claim on the God of the Israelites and call on his name (*cf* II Kings 5:17). But Daniel and his companions did not have even that. They were in a foreign land surrounded by foreign gods who, it was claimed, were completely in control. They were soon to discover, however, as believers have discovered in every generation, that God had gone on before and was well and truly settled in Babylon.

No land is foreign to him. He refuses to be stereotyped or to be confined within any land or nation, within any cult or culture, within any church or movement, within any liturgy or sacrament, within any confession or creed. He is wherever he chooses to be. He belongs to no one nation, no one culture, no one church, no one form of worship, no one doctrinal definition. He dwells in Jerusalem, but he is at home also in Babylon, Saviour and Judge of both, sovereign Lord of Heaven and Hell.

The second thing they demonstrated is the corollary of the first. It is that God's faithful people survive in Babylon, albeit sometimes through much trial and suffering. Daniel and his companions found a sympathetic supporter in Ashpenaz the eunuch. Thank God for kind and helpful pagans! But, Ashpenaz apart, the going was rough, as the rest of the book makes only too plain. It is true that the outcome of the story, like that of Job, is a happy one: they were 'ten times better than all the magicians ... and continued until the first year of King Cyrus' (Dan. 1:20*f*). But such a happy ending is never guaranteed to the children of God. The doctrine of 'believe and prosper' is a highly dangerous one ('only trust him and he will give you success in business') and is a denial of the Gospel of him who, in his temptations in the wilderness, rejected the way of affluence, success and worldly power, and on the cross suffered, bled and died.

God's people live in Babylon where God himself lives; but they know that that is not their true home. They know they are aliens in a foreign land and long for Jerusalem. The oft-quoted words of the *Epistle to Diognetus* put the situation in a nutshell.

> 'Christians are not distinguished from the rest of mankind
> either in locality or in speech or in customs ... While they dwell
> in cities of Greek and barbarians as the lot of each is cast, and
> follow the native customs in dress and food and the other
> arrangements of life, yet ... they dwell in their own countries,
> but only as sojourners, they bear their share in all things as
> citizens, and they endure all hardships as strangers. Every
> foreign country is a fatherland to them, and every fatherland
> is foreign ... Their existence is on earth, but their citizenship is
> in heaven ... They love all men ... and they are persecuted by
> all ... They are evil spoken of, and yet they are vindicated.
> They are reviled and they bless; they are insulted and they
> repent ... In a word, what the soul is in the body, this the
> Christians are in the world'
>
> (30–35).

They belong to this country and that; yet their true home is
another country, the city of God (*cf* Heb. 11:10), to which and
to whom they owe their ultimate allegiance. Life for the
people of God in Babylon is no sinecure. Nevertheless it is in
the purpose of God, and that cannot be a bad thing.

The third thing they demonstrated is that God's people
must bear their true witness in Babylon, difficult though that
may be. Their true home may be another country, but
Babylon is where they are and they must learn to make the
best of a bad job. Take their worship, for example. How was it
possible for them to 'sing the Lord's song in a foreign land'
(Ps. 137:4)? No doubt they felt like the men to whom
reference is made in this Psalm who, we are told, hung up
their lyres on the willows, and wept when they remembered
Zion (Ps. 137:1–2). That is, they could opt out of their
situation and form a religious huddle of their own, mourning
the past and thinking only of the good old days. Jeremiah, in
his letter to the exiles, warned them against such a spirit of
resignation. On the contrary they were to make Babylon their
home and 'seek the welfare of the city' to which they had been
taken (Jer. 29:7). Prayer would take the place of sacrifice;
God's Temple is wherever God is (*cf* John 4:20*ff*); their
witness would be not only in Jerusalem, but in Babylon and to
the ends of the earth (*cf* Acts 1:8).

Jeremiah's counsel was both difficult and dangerous, as the

Jews in Antiochus's day and the Christians in Paul's day were yet to find. The Christian Church, like the Jewish community before it, found itself in a state of tension, with pagan influences pressing in from every side. They were to be involved in the affairs of their nation and state and open to its culture; and yet they were not to become conformed to its ways. In their witness, as in their worship, they were to be distinctive, not only in what they *said*, but above all in what they *did* and in what they *were*.

The relationship between Christianity and culture remains an extremely difficult one, not only for missions and missionaries abroad, but also for the Church at home. Proclamation of the Gospel must take into serious account the environment and the culture which is being addressed and aim its message at an identifiable target. But in so doing it lays itself open to the dangers of syncretism, compromise or even betrayal of the faith. This applies to the missionary in an 'other faith' situation, trying to build on existing foundations. It applies also to the believer within an atheistic society, striving to be a good citizen, yet knowing he must obey God rather than men (*cf* Acts 5:29). And it applies no less to the believer in the capitalist West, resisting the encroachment of materialism and the corrosion of western 'culture':

> 'The world is too much with us; late and soon,
> Getting and spending, we lay waste our powers'.

> 'The first duty of the Church, and its greatest service to the world, is that it be in very deed the Church — confessing the true faith, committed to the fulfilment of the will of Christ, its only Lord, and united in him in a fellowship of love and service'.
>
> (*The Churches Survey their Task*, 1937, p 57)

Let the Church be the Church even in Babylon.

3 Educating the young

It was people, then, Nebuchadnezzar was after; especially young people. 'Bring ... youths without blemish, handsome

and skilful in all wisdom, endowed with knowledge, understanding learning, and competent to serve in the king's
palace, and to teach them the letters and language of the
Chaldeans' (Dan. 1:3*f*). Young people — but not just any
young people. They must be of the very best stock — good
looking, physically fit and mentally alert; knowledgeable and
with practical skills. Their training must be on a par with that
of the Chaldean wise men whose knowledge of astrology and
magical lore gave them influence with God and man. It was
with such young men that the future lay; and it was the future
that Nebuchadnezzar was interested in.

Antiochus had somewhat the same ideas about the youth of
his day. Not content with winning over the ruling priestly
class to his Hellenistic culture, he set about enlisting the
support of the young people. In city after city he set up
gymnasiums and athletic stadiums which were not just sport
centres but universities and polytechnics as well. Physical
fitness and mental agility must go hand in hand. The young
people came crowding in. Jews and Gentiles together. Par-
ticipation in heathen rituals at initiation ceremonies and the
like, many felt, was a small price to be paid by a Jewish lad to
have such an opportunity as this. And if, on the race track
where he ran naked, he was confronted by the derisive
whistles of the crowd, he could always arrange to conceal his
tell-tale mark of circumcision (*cf* I Macc. 1:15).

The future is always in the hands of the younger generation.
Such is the speed of progress today that professors of medicine
and other branches of science are often reckoned to be too
old for appointment at 40, and company directors who have
not 'made it' by 38 are thought to be 'over the top'. Young
people are a valuable investment (*cf* I Tim. 4:12) and education
is a priority. Physical fitness, knowledge of the world around,
wisdom in assessment and competence in business — these
and their like are all worthy aims. But Daniel and his
companions demonstrated that a sound mind in a healthy
body, good and desirable though these might be, were not
enough. It remains true that 'manners maketh man' and that
moral rectitude and spiritual maturity are to be prized above
all else. 'I appeal to you', says Paul, '... to present your bodies
as a living sacrifice, holy, acceptable to God, which is your

spiritual worship ... be transformed by the renewal of your mind, that you may prove what is the will of God, what is good and acceptable and perfect' (Rom. 12:1*f*).

4   A Three Years' Plan

Having chosen his young men, Nebuchadnezzar left nothing to chance. With great care he worked out a Three Years' Plan of education on the wisdom and culture of the Chaldeans. 'They were to be educated for three years' (Dan. 1:5). But, like Antiochus after him, he was much more interested in indoctrination than he was in education. To help in the process he offered them preferential treatment: 'the king assigned them a daily portion of the rich food which the king ate, and of the wine which he drank' (Dan. 1:5) and changed their religious identity by giving them Babylonian names incorporating the names of Babylonian gods: 'Daniel he called Belteshazzar, Hananiah he called Shadrach, Mishael he called Meshach, and Azariah he called Abednego' (Dan: 1:7).

And he is still at it. Not least in political and ideological circles where an open mind in an open society is looked upon with grave suspicion. Schools, universities, polytechnics and other places of higher education are all too often used to shape and, if needs be, to bend the minds of the young so that they will fit into his particular ideological scheme. Detention centres, 'corrective' courses and mental institutions are employed to break stubborn wills, whilst subliminal propaganda and brain-washing techniques can be relied upon to give outstanding results. Here too, as with Nebuchadnezzar, preferential treatment is still offered as an incentive — entry to higher education, advancement in employment, acceptance within the community — whilst a change of identity is always welcome, especially if it signifies a change of political allegiance or a denial of religious faith.

But indoctrination is not confined to the political or ideological scenes. It is to be found too in the religious sphere and is sometimes encouraged by the Church itself. The history of the Church is replete with accounts of bigotry and intolerance which can be traced back to its cultivation of the closed mind and its safeguarding of doctrine and tradition at the expense of freedom and truth. Nor is this confined to the past. Christian disunity and division are due, in no small measure, to preconceived ideas planted in a child's or the community's mind — ideas which reflect indoctrination rather than education, prejudice rather than trust. Such a price is surely too high to pay for the preferential treatment we may receive and is a denial of the name of the God we profess which is truth and love.

But things worked out differently for these young Jewish men from the way Nebuchadnezzar had expected, for 'they were better in appearance ... than all the youths' (Dan. 1:15). The proof of the pudding (even a vegetarian one) is in the eating of it. Daniel and his companions declined the king's rich fare and stuck to their simple diet of vegetables and water (Dan. 1:16). Nebuchadnezzer and his stewards were most pleasantly surprised. Not only were these young men superbly fit physically, they were ten times better than other youths in 'every matter of wisdom and understanding' (Dan. 1:20).

The story has nothing to do with the merits of vegetarianism and teetotalism, good though these may be in themselves. It has to do rather with the rights and wrongs of obeying Jewish dietary laws and of declining food which may have been offered first to idols. The point of the story would not be lost on the Jews of the second century BC, for to them this was an important point at issue. Obedience to dietary laws was much more than a culinary concern — it was a vitally important expression of their faith, to be taken most seriously along with the practice of circumcision and the observance of the Sabbath and other religious festivals. It was, as it were, an acted creed. As such it not only testified to their Jewish faith, it at the same time established them in it. Ritual is no substitute for righteousness, as the great prophets clearly remind us; but the faith, be it Jewish or Christian, would be much the poorer without it. It is when 'ritual' becomes 'mere ritual', and laws become bonds that true religion is in danger of betraying itself and its God.

Daniel and his friends were young men of principle. They were Hebrew youths owing allegiance to the God of their fathers. They had been loyal to him in Jerusalem; they would be loyal to him in Babylon also. And in acting as they did, their deeds spoke more loudly than their words. To act on principle is sometimes an expression of stubbornness and pig-headedness. But that is no excuse for denigrating the act itself. Men of principle find greater favour with God than do men of property. They are prepared to pay the price for the stand they take; they accept the penalty of being the odd man out; they are willing to be counted among the dissenters and the dissidents, whatever the outcome may be. When principle ceases to matter, then religion, truth, honesty and integrity are all at risk.

These Hebrew youths, having taken their stand on principle, were ready to submit themselves to a test for ten days living on vegetables and water: 'for ten days; let us be given vegetables to eat and water to drink' (Dan. 1:12). In the end they came through with flying colours and found favour with the king: 'none was found like Daniel, Hananiah, Mishael, and Azariah' (Dan. 1:19).

Sometimes the stand taken meets with favour; at other times with violent opposition. 'The Day', says Paul, 'will disclose it, because it will be revealed with fire, and the fire will test what sort of work each one has done' (I Cor. 3:13). But whatever the outcome, God is present through it all, and his favour is much more important than that of the king. 'By God's power [you] are guarded through faith for a salvation ready to be revealed in the last time. In this you rejoice, though now for a little while you may have to suffer various trials, so that the genuineness of your faith, more precious than gold which though perishable is tested by fire, may redound to praise and glory and honour at the revelation of Jesus Christ' (I Peter 1:5–7). Noble words for noble deeds!

2

A Bad Dream

1 Forgotten dreams

Nebuchadnezzar was not the first ruler to have bad dreams, nor will he be the last: 'his spirit was troubled, and his sleep left him' (Dan. 2:1). Would that they were more common than they are! There is enough injustice and oppression in our world to give many a ruler a sleepless night, but all too often they sleep peacefully in their beds, insensitive to the evil they do and the suffering they cause. There is no record that Nero had bad dreams over the burning of Rome, or Hitler over the Jewish holocaust, or Stalin over the Gulag Archipelago. Such dreams they left to their victims, dreams that suppurated into nightmares. Pray God more rulers will be given bad dreams, for then the oppressed may be spared those terrifying visions that appear in 'the dark watches of the night'.

At other times the dream comes as a warning, a presage of what might be if something is not done. The wise men in the nativity story, for example, were 'warned in a dream not to return to Herod', and so they returned to their home another way (Matt. 2:12). Joseph received a dream that the same Herod was about to search for the holy child to destroy him, and so he took his family to Egypt (Matt. 2:13*ff*). Nor can we forget Pilate's wife who warned her husband, 'Have nothing to do with that righteous man, for I have suffered much over him today in a dream' (Matt. 27:19). Warnings are there to be heeded. They may come by dreams or by some other means. But if they come from God, woe betide us if we pay no heed. Even bad dreams can come as revelations and lead to repentance.

The difficulty is that Nebuchadnezzar could not remember what his dream was about. 'Then the king commanded that the magicians, the enchanters, the sorcerers and the Chaldeans be summoned ... and the king said to them ... "I had a dream, and my spirit is troubled to know the dream"' (Dan. 2:2*f*). The only thing he could recall was that it was important and that it had come as a warning to him. But a warning of what? Of this he had no idea.

The mind, it is said, plays many strange tricks. So also does the subconscious. Sometimes we forget because deep down we want to forget. It is too much for the human psyche to bear and so the thought or the dream is obliterated from our awareness. But thoughts and dreams which are sent by God, even disturbing ones, cannot afford to be bottled up and stacked away in the cellars of the mind. They must be brought out into the open and be seen for what they are. Only then can they lose their mystery and be robbed of their terror. Only then can they become a vehicle of repentance and a means of response to the promptings and warnings of God's Spirit.

Having failed to recall his dream, then, for whatever reason, Nebuchadnezzar decided to call in the experts, the men whose job it was to deal with mysteries, who had been trained in astrology and sorcery and in all kinds of magic. But with all their training and erudition and 'know-how', they were unable to do a thing. They were to demonstrate all too clearly that there is a limit set to human wisdom.

How true it is that the more we know the more we know we don't know. Beyond discovery lie successive mysteries which human wisdom can never hope to understand. This is no less true of science than it is of religion. The mysteries of the molecule, like the mysteries of the vast universe, stretch out in endless line into the infinity of un-knowing. So too do the mysteries of the mind of God: 'Lo, these are but the outskirts of his ways; and how small a whisper do we hear of him! But the thunder of his power who can understand?' (Job 26:14).

2 Tyranny demands obedience

The result of all this was that 'the King was angry and very furious, and commanded that all the wise men of Babylon be destroyed' (Dan. 2:12). The wise men knew that what the king

asked was quite impossible. But that in no way inhibited the
king. It never does. As all-powerful ruler he expected the
impossible to be achieved, simply because he had commanded
it to be done. There was no point in the wise men arguing that
his request was altogether unreasonable. The question of
reasonableness just did not come into it at all. The request
that the king tell the dream and then they would give the
interpretation was itself interpreted as delaying tactics to save
their own skins: 'I know with certainty that you are trying to
gain time' (Dan. 2:8). His patience ran out. He was furious
and very angry (Dan. 2:12) and resorted to threats of the
most dire kind. He would tear them 'limb from limb' (Dan.
2:5). At the end of his tether, he called out Arioch, the captain
of the guard, and gave orders for their execution: 'he
commanded that all the wise men of Babylon be destroyed'
(Dan. 2:12).

Tyranny demands total obedience. There is no limit to
absolute power. It matters not if the demand is difficult or
even impossible. It must be carried out simply because the
powers-that-be demand it. To make excuses or to refuse is a
direct challenge to authority. Exasperation leads to bluster
and bluster to threats of violence and threats of violence to
the slaughter of the innocent. Adolf Hitler is a prime example
of this process. As soon as he was heard to say, 'My patience is
exhausted', the world knew what to expect. Bluster and
threats followed; then came the command to 'Arioch', captain
of the guard, to 'call out the troops'. The bombs fell on
Poland and the carnage had begun.

Violence so often erupts out of a fear of the unknown. Like
a self-breeding reactor, it feeds upon itself, grows out of
all proportion and leaves much dangerous waste behind. Kill
the wise men who show such intransigence and such in-
competence, and then go on to kill others like them, whether
they are personally involved or not. All must be destroyed.
Violence has a habit of gathering momentum at a frightening
rate. It begins by being destructive and ends by being self-
destructive. 'All who take the sword will perish by the sword'
(Matt. 26:52).

The threats of Nebuchadnezzar made no attempt to dis-
tinguish the guilty from the innocent; and Daniel and his

companions found themselves, embarrassingly to say the least, in the latter camp: 'they sought Daniel and his companions to slay them' (Dan. 2:13). Something had to be done, if only for the sake of self-preservation. With the executioners ready to strike, Daniel went straight to Arioch, not with bluster or yet with whining, but 'with prudence and discretion' (Dan. 2:14) and reasoned with him. As a result of Arioch's good offices, Daniel was shown into the presence of the king. Greatly daring, he begged the king to give him an appointment when, he promised, he would make known the dream and its interpretation (Dan. 2:16).

The man of God has sometimes to throw caution to the wind when he sees injustice being done to the innocent, whether he is personally involved or not, and has to 'stick his neck out'. This may mean, as in the case of Elijah for example, confronting the king (*cf* I Kings 21:17*ff*), and running the risk of imprisonment or even death. Such confrontation is sometimes dangerous and always difficult. But it is a duty which cannot be shirked.

Nor can the Church afford to kowtow to the State if evil is being perpetrated and the innocent made to suffer, whether they are 'of the faith' or not. There comes a time when its voice must be heard in the king's palace. It will speak with prudence and discretion, remembering the command of its Lord to be 'wise as serpents and innocent as doves' (Matt. 10:16); but it will speak too with firmness and conviction. Such a confrontation may not at first please the king and may be regarded as a challenge to authority or even as treason, as in the case of the prophet Jeremiah who suffered grievously as a so-called traitor to his king and country (*cf* Jer. 26:11). Such criticism, however, is a sign, not of treason or treachery or betrayal, but rather of true patriotism. That fact Nebuchadnezzar was ultimately to recognise.

3 Partners in prayer

'Then Daniel went to his house and made the matter known to ... his companions, and told them to seek mercy of the God of heaven concerning this mystery' (Dan. 2:17*f*). If Daniel was a man of action he was also a man of prayer. This will become even clearer in subsequent stories. Here he enlists the support of his friends and colleagues to join him in intercession that God will reveal the mystery of the dream and its interpretation so that their lives and the lives of many others will be spared.

This is perhaps the first reference in scripture to a 'house-group' meeting for prayer. In the New Testament, Christians are admonished not to neglect meeting together (*cf* Heb. 10:25) for fellowship, worship and prayer. More often than not this was done in the homes of believers. Like Daniel, they found encouragement in one another's company and enlisted the prayer-support of their fellow-believers. Prayer-partners, be they on the 'mission field' or at home, are a source of great spiritual power. But they have a responsibility in prayer not only for one another, but also for their nation and the other nations of the world. Intercessions are to be offered 'for kings and all who are in high positions, that we may live a quiet and peaceable life' (I Tim. 2:2). The Church has a responsibility to offer its united prayer that the kings of the earth will refrain from violence and seek the wisdom that only God can provide.

No sooner had he sought the prayer-support of his colleagues than 'the mystery was revealed to Daniel in a vision of the night' (Dan. 2:19). His reaction was two-fold: first of all he worshipped God and thanked him for answering his prayer, and second, he went to Arioch to do something about it. Prayer and action, worship and involvement must go together. In the prayer be blessed God simply for being God, the source of all wisdom and might, the disposer of kings and princes, the revealer of deep and unfathomable mysteries. It is this great and mysterious God, the God '[who] knows what is in the darkness and the light dwells with him' (Dan. 2:22), who had answered his prayer and made known to him the king's dream.

The Psalmist reminds us that 'the Lord of hosts' is also 'the God of Jacob' (Ps. 46:7); the God afar off is also the God near at hand (Jer. 23:23); 'Our Father who art in heaven' is the one who gives 'our daily bread' (Matt. 6:9*ff*); the 'Holy Father' (John 17:11) is the one to whom we can come with 'confidence' (Heb. 10:19) as to a God of love. To Daniel the transcendent God was the ever-present God who hears and answers prayer.

4 Divine wisdom

And now we come to the crux of the story. Daniel addresses Nebuchadnezzar: 'There is a God in heaven who reveals mysteries ... But as for me, not because of any wisdom that I have more than all the living has this mystery been revealed to me, but in order that the interpretation may be made known to the king' (Dan 2: 28, 30). The purpose of the story is to demonstrate that the wisdom of God is far superior to the wisdom of the Chaldean sages, and by the same token that the wisdom of Daniel's people is far superior to that of their sophisticated critics. The God of Daniel is their God; he reveals to his people mysteries which the wisest of men cannot even begin to understand. But let them not forget that the wisdom they possess is not simply the product of their own minds and imaginations, for in themselves they are no wiser than the Gentiles around them. Their wisdom comes from none other than 'God in heaven who reveals mysteries' (Dan. 2:28).

The Apostle Paul was to remind the church in Corinth of the self-same things. Quoting from the prophecy of Isaiah he says, 'I [God] will destroy the wisdom of the wise, and the cleverness of the clever I will thwart' (I Cor. 1:19; see Isa. 29:14). The Christian community in Corinth may be overawed by Greek oratory and Greek sophistry and by its dazzling display of intellect and erudition. But this gathering of humble folk must feel no inferiority when confronted by Greek wisdom. God has given them a wisdom that is far superior to that of their neighbours. It is to be found in the story of the crucified Christ through whom men and women may find salvation. The Greeks may call it sheer folly; but let them be assured that the foolishness of God is wiser than men (1 Cor. 1:21). Through the folly of what is preached God has 'made foolish the wisdom of the world' (I Cor. 1:20). And as with Daniel so also with them, the wisdom they possess, which gives insight into the very mind and purpose of God, is not of their own contriving; it is none other than a revelation from God himself. For this reason there is no room for boasting on their part. On the contrary, as it is written, 'Let him who boasts, boast of the Lord' (I Cor. 1:30).

The wisdom of which Daniel speaks gives profound insight into the mysteries of God, and not least into the mystery of the age to come. The mystery contained in Nebuchadnezzar's dream concerns 'what will be in the latter days' (Dan. 2:28). In the New Testament the word appears quite frequently, but there it signifies not so much an unsolved mystery concerning the future as an open secret, a mystery whose meaning has already been disclosed by Jesus Christ, the Son of God, the Alpha and the Omega, the Beginning and the End (*cf* Rev. 1:8). 'To you', says Jesus to his disciples, 'has been given the secret of the kingdom of God, but for those outside everything is in parables' (Mark 4:11). And the secret of that kingdom is to be found in the person of Jesus himself. This was a mystery which was kept secret for a long time, but was now disclosed (Rom. 11:25); it is none other than 'the plan ... hidden for ages in God who created all things' (Eph. 3:9) which is 'Christ in you, the hope of glory' (Col. 1:27). The mystery of God's purpose for all the ages, whose meaning is made known only by God-given wisdom, is uncovered by Jesus in his teaching, in his healing and above all in his cross and resurrection. Here is something that no human wisdom could ever have discovered by itself. It is a mystery of salvation through suffering, of life through death. It is a revelation from above which will find its final confirmation in the last times when he, our Lord, will be vindicated before the eyes of the world (*cf* Rev. 1:7). The crucified and risen Christ is both 'the power of God and the wisdom of God' (I Cor. 1:24).

This open secret moreover has been made known to those whom God has called, and it is incumbent upon them, as it was upon Daniel, to bear witness to what they have received. This they will do, not only by the testimony of their mouths, but also by their readiness to 'share his sufferings' (Phil. 3:10). The witness is at the same time the martyr: 'He showed them his hands and his side [saying] ... "As the Father has sent me, even so I send you"' (John 20:21*ff*). His mission is our mission; his marks are our marks; his joy is our joy (*cf* John 20:22).

5 A frightening image

The moment the king and his wise men had been waiting for has now arrived: 'You saw, O king, and behold, a great image' (Dan. 2:31). Here, then, is the content of the forgotten dream, and here is its interpretation. It concerns a frightening image, a colossal figure with 'head ... of fine gold, its breast and arms of silver, its belly and thighs of bronze, its legs of iron, its feet partly of iron and partly of clay' (Dan. 2.32*f*). A mysterious stone smites the feet and shatters them in pieces with the result that the whole image comes crashing down, is pulverised and scattered by the wind. The stone itself becomes a great mountain and fills the whole earth (Dan. 2.34*f*).

It was quite customary in the Middle East at that time for nations to be described by the symbolism of metals. Their most likely identification here may be that the gold stands for Babylon (with Nebuchadnezzar as its king), the silver for Media, the bronze for Persia, and the iron and the iron mixed with clay for Alexander's Greece and its Ptolemaic and Seleucid successors.

For our purpose, however, the identification of the various metals hardly matters at all. The dream serves to demonstrate that, just as their God is superior to all the other gods of the nations in wisdom, so also is he superior in power. The Gentile nations present a frightening image indeed. It is true that since the time of Nebuchadnezzar their kingdoms had deteriorated from gold down to the vulnerable feet of clay. But the picture was still a frightening one for the small, crushed and subservient people of God.

The dream declares, however, that despite all appearances to the contrary, there is no cause to fear, for the God in whom they trust is in control of history and is able to humble the proud and the powerful. It matters not to him whether they are gold or clay, the time will come when all the kingdoms of the earth will crumble to dust. There is a unity in history — past, present and future — within which the writer of Daniel sees the working out of the divine purpose, culminating in the fast-approaching End. But there is also a judgment in history in which, in the words of Herbert Butterfield:

'the sentence falls on great human systems, on nations, civilisa-
tions, institutions; indeed on all the schematised patterns into
which human life ranges itself in various periods. The systems
break, the organisations crumble'.

(Christianity and History, 1949, pp 60, 64).

Such belief in the purpose of God in history and in divine
judgment upon history is, of course, an act of faith in
response to the revelation of God in Christ in whom all things
hold together (Col. 1:17), and through whom mankind is
judged (John 5:22).

Having described the dream, Daniel now addresses himself
respectfully to the king: 'You, O king, the king of kings, to
whom the God of heaven has given the kingdom, the power,
and the might, and the glory, and into whose hand he has
given, wherever they dwell, the sons of men, the beasts of the
field and the birds of the air, making you rule over them all —
you are the head of gold' (Dan 2: 37*f*). The writer of Daniel
asserts that the authority possessed by Nebuchadnezzar has
been given to him by none other than God himself. In this he
is in agreement with the prophet Jeremiah, for example,
speaking in the name of God: 'It is I who by my great power
and my outstretched arm have made the earth, with the men
and animals that are on the earth, and I give it to whomever
seems right to me. Now I have given all these lands into the
hand of Nebuchadnezzar, the king of Babylon, my servant,
and I have given him also the beasts of the field to serve him'
(Jer. 27:5*f*). Nebuchadnezzar is God's 'servant', as Cyrus is
God's 'anointed' (Isa. 45:1).

'There is no authority,' writes the Apostle Paul, 'except
from God, and those that exist have been instituted by God'
(Rom. 13:1). There is a place in the providence and purpose
of God for king and subjects, ruler and ruled, state and
citizen. But, that having been said, the Nebuchadnezzars of
this world have no divine right to rule as if they themselves
were gods. Such authority as they possess has been given to
them in trust from him who is Lord of lords and King of
kings. Whether they acknowledge him or not, they are
responsible to him for the way they use their power and for
the way they abuse it. Dominion does not imply domination.

They will be judged, not by a divine right to do as they please, but by a divine mandate to establish righteousness and peace in the earth. The God who builds and plants is the same God who plucks up and destroys (Jer. 1:10). Nebuchadnezzar's dominion, however glorious and golden, is for a short time only and will come to an end according to the purpose of the God of heaven who rules over all things.

The question of the limits of secular authority has always raised problems for the Christian Church, not least today. In certain atheistic states, for example, a constant point of debate among Christians has been the relationship between the words of Romans 13:1: 'Let every person be subject to the governing authorities', and those of Acts 5:29: 'We must obey God rather than men'. When do we do the one and when do we do the other? Authority is delegated to men by God and is given to whomever he wills; but it belongs first and last to him. There are times, however, when his divine mandate is flouted or denied and God's servant becomes the beast which, by its very exercise of authority, blasphemes the name of God (*cf* Rev. 13:1). Peter Crassus had something pertinent to say in this regard: 'Render to Caesar the things that are Caesar's, but not to Tiberius the things that are Tiberius's, for Caesar is good, but Tiberius is bad'. Daniel's judgment is equally pertinent: 'the iron, the clay, the bronze, the silver, and the gold, all together were broken in pieces, and became like the chaff of the summer threshing floors' (Dan. 2:35). The mills of God grind slowly, but they grind exceedingly small.

6 A miraculous stone

The agent of the divine judgment is a mysterious stone 'cut out by no human hand, and it smote the image on its feet ... The stone that struck the image became a great mountain and filled the whole earth ... The God of heaven will set up a kingdom that will never be destroyed, nor shall its sovereignty be left to another people' (Dan. 2:34*f*, 44). A miraculous stone breaks loose and smashes the image in pieces and, in a way that can happen only in dreams, becomes a great mountain. The interpretation given is that this stone represents a fifth kingdom, the kingdom of God, which will bring to an end the kingdoms of this world and exercise its universal rule from the earth's centre in Mount Zion.

Little is said about the nature of this kingdom. But this at least is clear: it is God's kingdom 'cut from a mountain by no human hand' (Dan. 2:45), it destroys and replaces the kingdoms of this earth (Dan. 2:44), and it is universal and eternal in its scope (Dan. 2:35, 44). The writer of Daniel lived in troublous times when men yearned for the destruction of Antiochus and all his ways and for the coming of God's kingdom. Later on, in the time of Roman rule, the Zealots sought to force the hand of history and bring in the kingdom by force. There is no hint of such measures here, however. God would bring it about in his own good time.

This vision of the miraculous stone, representing the fifth kingdom which will destroy the kingdoms of the earth, has inspired not a few attempts to overthrow the powers-that-be. In seventeenth century England, for example, in the time of Oliver Cromwell, a small Puritan sect arose calling itself *The Fifth Monarchy Movement*, which saw in Cromwell's government a preparation for the 'fifth monarchy' in which Christ would reign in his kingdom for a thousand years. Disillusioned by Cromwell's rule, a group of them marched on London in 1661, but were routed and their leaders killed. The writer of Daniel refused to anticipate God's kingdom by force of arms or any other means of human contriving. That kingdom, he believed, would come in God's good time and in God's appointed way.

7   Promotion

And so the story ends, with the vindication of our hero and the conversion of the king: 'Truly, your God is God of gods and Lord of kings ... Then the king gave Daniel high honours and many great gifts, and made him ruler over the whole province of Babylon' (Dan 2:47*f*). It is a feature of folk-tales that the hero is vindicated and that he and the others live happily ever after. So it is here. Nebuchadnezzar honours Daniel and acknowledges Daniel's God. Would that it were always so. But history and experience speak otherwise. Rulers continue to blaspheme, and the faithful continue to suffer. Judgment on evil is not always instant, and faithfulness is not always rewarded with high honours. On the contrary, the powerful continue to prosper and the powerless are trodden underfoot. But the promise remains that in God's good time the meek shall inherit the earth (Matt. 5:5), for in the providence of God 'the weakness of God is stronger than men' (I Cor. 1:25).

3

Fear and Fire

1   The golden image

Here Nebuchadnezzar does not just dream of an idol as in chapter 2, he actually makes one — a huge golden statue, 90 feet tall — and sets it up in the Plain of Dura for everyone to see. Let all his subjects bow down and worship it on pain of death (Dan. 3:1,5). And this is what he has been doing ever since, from the days of Antiochus and Nero right down to the days of Hitler and Stalin. Bow down — or else. In whatever age, the trouble with Nebuchadnezzar is that he is never content with plain obedience; he demands worship (Dan. 3:6,11). Herein, says Karl Barth, is the supreme act of sacrilege — when the ruler or the state or whatever demands of its subjects not just obedience, but love. No doubt the three young men in this story live as exemplary citizens of Babylon; but there are limits beyond which the faithful worshipper of God cannot go.

Throughout their history the Jews have been particularly vulnerable, for from the beginning they have set their faces resolutely against idolatry of every kind, be it the worship of an idol or the deification of a ruler or the glorification of a state. So too have the Christians. In Roman times they were actually charged with the crime of atheism because they refused to worship the accepted gods. In modern times the deities are different, but the demands are the same — bow down and worship. But the golden image, by whatever name, is still an idol, and idols have no claim to the worship that is due to God and to God alone.

Nebuchadnezzar, we note, seeks the maximum publicity for what he does. He chooses the Plain of Dura to set up his idol. Nothing must obstruct the people's view; the statue has

40

to be seen from miles around. Ignorance of the law cannot be offered as an excuse. A great service of dedication is arranged to which all the chief dignitaries in the land are invited. Over and over again the list is read out of their impressive offices as if to emphasise the supreme importance of the occasion: 'the satraps, the prefects, and the governors, the counsellors, the treasurers, the justices, the magistrates and all the officials of the provinces' (Dan 3: 2,3). The drums roll, the trumpets blare and the great massed bands come crashing in: 'the sound of the horn, pipe, lyre, trigon, harp, bagpipe, and every kind of music' (Dan. 3: 5,7,10,15). Martial music fills the air as the people are conditioned for the great event. The cord is pulled, the statue is unveiled and the people prostrate themselves in worship before the splendour of the golden image.

Nebuchadnezzar always likes to make a show when dedicating his idol which is often more impressive and awe-inspiring than the one set up on the Plain of Dura. Sometimes it is gold-plated all over, a beneficent god who guarantees security and showers lavish riches on all his devotees: 'Bow down and worship, and I will give you ...'. At other times it assumes the shape of a mighty warrior, bristling with weapons, surrounded by tanks, guns, rockets and a bewildering array of sophisticated armoury, demonstrating his fearful power and his ability to crush all opposition to his will. An awe-inspiring spectacle indeed.

2   The fiery furnace

To impress his will on the people, Nebuchadnezzar uses many different ploys. But by far the most prized weapons in his arsenal are those of threat and fear. He gives his peremptory command and all the officials jump to attention: 'they stood before the image that Nebuchadnezzar had set up' (Dan. 3:3). Then comes the threat: those who disobey his command to worship the image will be thrown into 'a burning fiery furnace' (Dan. 3:6).

Fear is a terrifying weapon, and Nebuchadnezzar knows how to use it. He builds up the people's terror as he stokes up the heat of the furnace. Behind the sound of martial music his would-be victims can detect a requiem. They know a strong man when they see one, and Nebuchadnezzar is a strong man. He has but to speak a word only and the deed is done. He holds in his hands the power of life and of death. Wherever he goes he takes his fiery furnace with him, glowing white hot, with its flames leaping high into the night sky (see the apocryphal *Prayer of Azariah*, verse 24).

The moving story of the seven brothers recorded in II Maccabees 7 graphically illustrates the fate of many Jews in the time of the tyrant Antiochus: 'The king fell into a rage and gave orders that pans and cauldrons be heated ... When he [the first brother] was utterly helpless, the king ordered them to take him to the fire, still breathing, and to fry him in a pan' (II Macc. 7:3*ff*). In a later century the Christians were to suffer a somewhat similar fate. Refusing to worship the Roman emperor, they were dressed in animal skins and thrown into the arena to be mauled by wild beasts; they were dipped in boiling tar and set alight to brighten up the imperial gardens.

And still the furnace rages. At the close of the war I saw that furnace in a place called Auschwitz, the notorious concentration camp near Cracow in Poland, where unbelievably four million people died, many of them, if not most of them, Jews. I was quite unprepared for what I saw that day. I stood in the gas chamber where the deadly crystals of hydrogen cyanide were poured in from an opening above. I looked into the incinerators where body after body was catapulted into the furnace as from the breech of a gun. I saw the obscene sight of human hair — mountains of it — preserved for mattresses or the making of suits of clothes; tens of thousands of tangled metal spectacles; thousands of sets of dentures; hundreds of artificial limbs; bowls, basins and chamber-pots — all the private intimacies of innocent people who happened to be Jews or whose political or religious convictions had failed to pass the test. And all this was done, I was told, to the sound of music, whilst the gaolers stood to attention before the golden image that Nebuchadnezzar had set up.

The fear inspired by Nebuchadnezzar takes many different forms — exile, prison, forced labour, disappearance, torture, psychiatric ward. 'In recent years', says an authoritative report from the World Council of Churches, 'the incidents of gross violations of the crudest and most inhuman type have multiplied to an extent unparalleled in human history.' In scores of countries at this present time the gross violation of both civil and social rights has reached epidemic proportions. And prominent among such violations is that of religious freedom, as the many stories of modern martyrs so eloquently testify. The claims of religious faith, be they Jewish or Christian, are still a challenge to Nebuchadnezzar and his golden image. To them there is only one God, and him only will they serve.

Fear of the furnace is still used as a powerful threat, and would-be dissidents — political and religious alike — are warned to beware. But there is an antidote that resists all such threats and quells our fears. It is that faith that can quench fires as well as move mountains, faith in the power and the love of God. In the Prayer of Azariah it is said that the three young men 'walked about in the midst of the flames, singing hymns to God and blessing the Lord' (verse 1). In the same way, we are told, Paul and Silas in prison 'were praying and singing hymns to God, and the prisoners were listening to them' (Acts 16:25). And the same thing happens again today as a recent report of the trial of a Christian prisoner makes plain: 'The sentence was announced (five years in prison to be followed by five years' exile). When it was read out to them and they asked, "Have you understood?", he said, "Yes, glory to Jesus Christ." The whole courtroom clapped, they applauded and laughed. His daughter climbed on to a seat and said, "Father, with Christ you are free in prison; freedom without him is prison" ... There were more than 500 believers outside the building. Removing their headgear, they began to sing, and the song they sang was *For the sake of the Gospel.*'

'We know and believe the love God has for us', writes John. 'God is love, and he who abides in love abides in God, and God abides in him ... There is no fear in love, but perfect love casts out fear' (I John 4:16, 18). When the drums and the trumpets cease, there is heard the triumphant song of praise.

3   The informers

Knowing human nature as we do, we are not surprised at the way the story unfolds: 'At that time certain Chaldeans came forward and maliciously accused the Jews' (Dan. 3:8). It always pays, it is said, to keep in with those in power; and the Chaldeans were no exception — they reported the young Jewish men to the king. The political or religious informer who spies on his friends and reports them to the authorities is a despicable character. Judas did it with a kiss and in return for 30 pieces of silver (*cf* Matt. 26:15,48). Others have done it for less or simply to curry favour with their lords and masters. Others again have done it out of spite or envy or both. In the case of the Chaldeans, who were the young men's colleagues, it was done out of malice. The fact that what they said was true does not exonerate them one little bit. To betray a friend is a contemptible act, deserving of the utmost condemnation.

And yet the fact is that we have all acted despicably, sometimes openly and blatantly, but more often covertly and secretly. We have not stooped to inform on another, but we have betrayed our trust, if not in deed then in thought, if not in act then in intention. And more often than not the object of our betrayal is the most vulnerable and so the outcome has been the most tragic. Friendship is a sacred relationship which bears the divine seal. To betray that friendship, to besmirch that love is to deny a divine trust and to give our allegiance to another god. 'There are friends who pretend to be friends, but there is a friend who sticks closer than a brother' (Prov. 18:24). 'When my father and my mother forsake me, then the Lord will take me up' (Ps. 27:10, *Authorised Version*). Thank God for loyal friends — and thank God for God.

4   The Great Power

Nebuchadnezzar's general warning now becomes a personal threat: 'if you do not worship, you shall immediately be cast into a burning fiery furnace' (Dan. 3:15). It is relatively easy to remain cool and detached when we are not personally involved but just one of the crowd. It can't happen to us! But things take on a totally different complexion when we are singled out from the crowd and made to stand alone before the judge. We can feel the heat of the furnace already on our faces and we begin to perspire, with apprehension if not with the heat itself.

But what really riles these three young men is not Nebuchadnezzar's threat of the furnace, but rather his denigration of their God: 'Who is the god that will deliver you out of my hands?' (Dan. 3:15). The greatest temptation of power is to imagine that it is the Great Power (*cf* Acts 8:10); and the greatest temptation of tyrants is to imagine that they are gods. Nebuchadnezzar was not a tyrant, though in this scene he comes very close to being one. A more obvious example would no doubt spring to the minds of the book's first readers, none other than Antiochus who actually assumed the title *Epiphanes* — '(God) Manifest'. The wags of that day called him, not Epiphanes, but Epimanes meaning 'madman'. But it was no joke, either for them or for the three young men. When tyrants or madmen claim to be gods, there is trouble brewing for those who stand in their way. The twentieth century, like many before it, has produced more than its fair share of tyrants and madmen who, by their actions if not by their words, have claimed to be God and have used the threat of the fiery furnace to force compliance with their will. They would do well to remember that:

'the sentence falls heaviest on those who come to think themselves gods, who fly in the face of Providence and history, who put their trust in man-made systems and worship the work of their own hands.'

(Herbert Butterfield, *ibid*, p. 60).

5   An affirmation of faith

In times of crisis, threat or tragedy God has a habit of calling out his 'righteous remnant' to bear witness to him. So it was at the time of the Flood. So it was also at the time of the exile — three young men, alone of 'all the peoples, nations and languages' (Dan. 3:7), refuse to fall down and worship the golden image. Their response to Nebuchadnezzar is a remarkable confession of faith: 'O Nebuchadnezzar, we have no need to answer you in this matter. If it be so, our God whom we serve is able to deliver us from the burning fiery furnace; and he will deliver us out of your hand, O king. But if not, be it known to you, O king, that we will not serve your gods or worship the golden image which you have set up' (Dan. 3:16–18).

There is no need for argument or excuse or special pleading. The young men speak with simplicity and conviction what they believe has been given them to say from above. As God's servants they have no need to enter into verbal controversy with the king. They speak what they know and testify to what they have seen (*cf* John 3:11) — that their God is indeed able to deliver them out of the king's hands and from the flames of the fiery furnace. It is an assertion that God is greater than Nebuchadnezzar and more powerful than circumstance.

We are reminded of Jesus' words to his disciples: 'Take heed to yourselves; for they will deliver you up to councils ... and you will stand before governors and kings for my sake ... And when they bring you to trial and deliver you up, do not be anxious beforehand what you are to say; but say whatever is given you in that hour, for it is not you who speak, but the Holy Spirit' (Mark 13:9*ff*).

Here is a picture of the Confessing Church at its best. As testimony after testimony has declared: 'By the power that works within us [he] is able to do far more abundantly than all that we ask or think' (Eph. 3:20).

Then comes this most moving affirmation: 'But if not ... we will not serve your gods' (Dan 3: 18). It is not the 'if not' of doubt; it is the 'if not' of supreme faith in a God who, despite all appearances to the contrary, 'is able for all time to save those who draw near to ... him' (Heb. 7:25). 'Blessed are those who have not seen and yet believe' (John 20:29). Here is an illustration of that 'disinterested religion' which trusts in God, not for what it will receive in return, but quite simply for his own sake. It recognises that, though God is indeed able to deliver from the fiery furnace, his faithful people may not in the event be spared that ordeal and may have to face its terrifying flames. But even if this be the case, they will not doubt either his power or his love.

This story, then, does not present trust in God as some kind of insurance policy against suffering or pain or death. For the Christian the witness of Jesus and his cross is the ultimate rebuttal of any such belief. The assurance given is that, though the flames of the furnace may do their worst, God's purpose will yet be fulfilled in resurrection. 'By his great mercy,' writes Peter, 'we have been born anew to a living hope through the resurrection of Jesus Christ from the dead' (I Peter 1:3). Thanks be to God.

6   Ordeal by fire

Nebuchadnezzar is not accustomed to being addressed in this way. The stand the young men take and the claims made by the king are mutually exclusive. Their words of defiance are a direct challenge to his authority and cannot be overlooked. His position is at stake; so too is that of his kingdom. State and Church, as it were, are on a collision course. The Church must be taught a lesson. It may appear to be quite insignificant over against the state — a pygmy over against a colossus. But no risks can be taken. Too much is at stake. It must be subjected to ordeal by fire.

The challenge of religion generates in tyrants a great deal of heat, in more ways than one, and leads to excesses they might perhaps have avoided in their saner moments: 'then Nebuchadnezzar was full of fury, and the expression of his face was changed' (Dan. 3:19). So furious is his anger that he gives the young men no time to prepare to meet their fate, no time even to change their clothes. Without delay he calls in his strong-armed men to throw the culprits into the flames. But in so doing they themselves are burnt alive (*cf* Dan. 3:20*ff*). Strong-armed men do not always meet such a fate. But Nebuchadnezzar has a habit of acting as he does here, with a passion out of all proportion to the nature of the crime committed. This is particularly so where matters of religion are concerned. The plea for religious liberty seems to touch a nerve that many other pleas do not. Sentences laid down for religious crimes have often a measure of severity difficult to justify or even to understand. Perhaps it has something to do with one of the earliest of all temptations — 'you will be like God' (Gen. 3:5). When an all-powerful, self-styled god-like man is confronted by a vulnerable manlike God, he immediately feels threatened and lashes out impulsively. But still the stand is taken and the confession made: 'we will not serve your gods or worship the golden image that you have set up' (Dan 3:18).

7   The fourth man

At this point in the story, suddenly and dramatically, there is introduced a reference, both mystical and mysterious, that causes the king to cry out in utter amazement: 'Did we not cast three men bound into the fire? ... But I see four men loose, walking in the midst of the fire, and they are not hurt; and the appearance of the fourth is like a son of the gods' (Dan. 3:24f). The writer of Daniel believes in miracles, because he believes that the spiritual realm is only a hand's breadth away. He believes too in angels, as witnesses to that reality and as agents of the Most High God. He believes in divine intervention, not least in the fiery furnace. He believes that God is ready to identify himself with his people in the times of their deepest need.

It is not surprising that, from its earliest days, the Christian Church has seen in this 'fourth man', not an angelic 'son of the gods', but the incarnate Son of God who, more than any other, identified himself with us and exposed himself to death on our behalf. Nor did he pass through that fiery ordeal unscathed. An early heresy would have had it otherwise — the divine Christ left the body of the man Jesus before the crucifixion (so that it was only a man who died) and was reunited with it at the resurrection. Such teaching was utterly condemned as the sheerest heresy. The Son of Man who was yet Son of God lived and died and rose again, sharing the threat of death with his people that they might share with him the promise of his resurrection. By his resurrection he assured them that death would have no dominion over them (*cf* Rom. 6:9). In the leaping flames of the furnace we see the shape of a cross and beyond that a garden with an empty tomb.

The same lesson of God's care and protection is conveyed

dramatically in the verses that follow: 'the fire had not had any power over the bodies of those men; the hair of their heads was not singed, their mantles were not harmed, and no smell of fire had come upon them' (Dan. 3:27). The early readers of the Book of Daniel, enduring trials and persecution and the threat of death, knew only too well that such miracles happened more often in fables than in fact. The moving stories in II Maccabees of the martyrdoms of Eleazar and of the seven brothers (*cf* 6:18–31; 7:1–42) would have had for them a familiar ring. They knew that to be thrown into the fiery furnace meant certain death — they had seen it happen to so many of their own friends and companions and knew it could quite easily happen to them also. And yet this story of the three young men brought with it an assurance and a hope that strengthened their resolve and helped them to face any fiery ordeal with total commitment.

The story declares loud and clear, not that God will save his people from the furnace, but that he will save them *in* the furnace. There are spiritual forces at work in this world that are greater by far than the power of Nebuchadnezzar. There are chariots and horsemen round about God's people that no human eye can see (*cf* II Kings 6:17). The spiritual world is much nearer than we think. Here indeed is ground for hope — a hope based not on fantasy but on faith, not on folklore but on the promise of the Son of God who not only faced death but also conquered death through his resurrection: 'When you pass through the waters I will be with you; and through the rivers, they shall not overwhelm you; when you walk through fire you shall not be burned, and the flame shall not consume you, For I am the Lord your God, the Holy One of Israel, your Saviour' (Isa. 43:2*f*).

The real miracle here is not that these young men came out of the furnace unscathed, but that they were willing in the first place to risk its flames.

4

A Great Tree

1   An everlasting kingdom

Nebuchadnezzar writes an epistle 'to all peoples, nations and languages' (Dan. 4:1) in which he describes a dream that terrifies him with its signs and wonders (Dan. 4:2). The effect on him is such that it brings him to acknowledge that '[God's] dominion is an everlasting dominion' (Dan. 4:34) and that God is sovereign Lord over all. Nebuchadnezzar's own kingdom, though powerful and great, is transient in the extreme and subject to the judgment of the Most High. Such recognition by the king may be no more than a piece of wishful thinking on the part of the writer of Daniel, for there is no historical evidence that he ever embraced the Jewish faith or accepted as his own the Jewish God. Nevertheless it expresses the writer's deeply felt conviction that God's kingdom will in the end triumph and God's people will be vindicated even in the eyes of their enemies.

This conviction has been shared by successive generations of those who have suffered for their faith, Jew and Christian alike. The 'signs of the times' may be dark indeed; the forces of evil may seem altogether invincible. But the tribulation will lead on to the kingdom. For the Christian believer this is more than wishful thinking or self-deception. The oft-sung litany, 'We shall overcome ... some day', is more than just 'whistling in the dark to keep our spirits up'. It is more than a forlorn hope based on an empty dream that somehow, somewhere, something will turn up. Rather, it is a living hope well and truly founded on the fact of the resurrection of Jesus Christ from the dead (cf I Peter 1:3). The time will come, says the Apostle Paul, when 'at the name of Jesus every knee shall bow ... and every tongue confess that Jesus Christ is Lord, to the glory of God the Father' (Phil. 2:10). This also is the confident hope of John on the isle of Patmos, for whom 'the tribulation and the kingdom' are inseparably bound together (Rev. 1:9). Contrary to all appearances, the day will soon dawn when 'every eye will see him, every one who pierced him; and all tribes of the earth will wail on account of him' (Rev. 1:7). It is a hope that looks yearningly to the future for its fulfilment; yet in Jesus that future hope is already a present reality. The coming kingdom has arrived — tomorrow is here; promise and fulfilment have joined hands; the 'future inheritance' is already sealed by the Holy Spirit who is the guarantee of what is yet to be (*cf* II Cor. 1:22; Eph. 1:14).

2   Call in the astrologers

Nebuchadnezzar, however, has to learn his lesson the hard way. He is 'at ease in [his] house and prospering in [his] palace' (Dan 4:4), when the sentence of judgment falls upon him. He is feeling utterly contented with his lot and thoroughly pleased with himself — a vulnerable position to be in, for it is when things look good that we often have cause to be most worried. At that very moment the unexpected happens: his tranquillity is shattered by 'a dream which made [him] afraid' (Dan. 4:5). Dreams can be fragile things that break up and dissolve with the rising of the sun. But they can also trouble and alarm if there is cause to think that they are premonitions of evil or indications of misfortune.

Unlike the dream in chapter 2, the contents of this one are vividly clear. What puzzles the king is its interpretation. As on the previous occasion he consults the magicians, the enchanters, the Chaldeans, but adds to their number the astrologers (Dan. 4:7). The attitude of Jewish writers at this time to astrology is ambivalent, but for the most part it is condemned as an evil thing, having been taught to men, it was believed, by one of the fallen angels (*cf* I En. 8:3), and is to be avoided at all costs as 'erroneous, such as foolish men enquire into day by day' (Sib. Or. 3.218). Despite such warnings, however, astrology continues to exercise a strange fascination over the minds of millions of people in these modern times. To many it is only an innocent pastime; but to others it has become a deeply entrenched superstition which is surely a denial of the sovereignty of God whose providential care is over all his creatures. To resort to magicians, enchanters and astrologers is a form of idolatry, inimical to faith in the one, true and only God.

3   A benevolent despot

The dream that so troubles Nebuchadnezzar concerns 'a tree in the midst of the earth; and its height was great. The tree grew and became strong, and its top reached to heaven, and it was visible to the end of the whole earth. Its leaves were fair and its fruit abundant, and in it was food for all. The beasts of the field found shade under it, and the birds of the air dwelt in its branches, and all flesh was fed from it' (Dan. 4:10–12). This tree is none other than Nebuchadnezzar himself who has grown and become strong and who has dominion to the ends of the earth (Dan. 4:22). It illustrates what he has always wanted to be — a world-famous ruler, the benefactor of his people and indeed of all mankind, a great father-figure dolling out largesse to all and sundry, a refuge to the outcast, a blessing to the poor. Fame and fortune would be his, with a reputation to match. His kingdom would cover the whole earth, and all mankind would be his debtor, grateful to be recipients of his favour. But such noble sentiments are not unalloyed, for they are motivated by a sense of his own importance and fed by his insatiable pride which, he is soon to discover, will bring down upon him the wrath of God.

Throughout the centuries many benevolent and not-so-benevolent despots have followed in Nebuchadnezzar's train, convinced too that they are God's great gift to mankind, prepared to ride rough-shod over their fellows for their own good. They have convinced themselves, and are determined to convince others, that their system of government, their culture, their tradition, their ideology is the answer to all their problems. Their fatherland, their motherland, has been destined to rule the earth and will usher in the Golden Age. If the price to be paid for such enlightenment is revolution, bloodshed or oppression, it is not too much for such a prize. In the end Nebuchadnezzar will be recognised as the saviour of the people, the father of the nation, the lord of creation itself.

The tree grows until it fills the whole earth; the birds and the beasts find shelter in its branches; its fruits are abundant and provide food for all. But unfortunately its leaves are not for the healing of the nations (Rev. 1:2). It blossoms and flourishes, but the difficulty is that in the shade of its mighty boughs little else can grow. Liberty and truth are particularly conspicuous by their absence. The price to be paid for such food and shelter is high indeed.

There is one tree, however, in whose shade liberty and truth and a thousand other fruits are free to flourish. It is a tree 'like a grain of mustard seed which ... when it has grown it is the greatest of shrubs and becomes a tree, so that the birds of the air come and make nests in its branches' (Matt. 13:31–32). The kingdom of God, for such it is, can alone bring such blessings to all mankind.

4 The watcher's warning

In his dream Nebuchadnezzar sees clearly a 'watcher, a holy one, [who] came down from heaven. He cried aloud and said thus, "Hew down the tree and cut off its branches, strip off its leaves and scatter its fruit; let the beasts flee from under it and the birds from its branches"' (Dan. 4:13*f*). An angel-messenger, whose task it is to watch over the affairs of God, suddenly appears and gives orders for the mighty tree to be hewn down. The king's overweening pride, despite his good intentions and philanthropic dreams, has brought down upon him and his kingdom the awful judgment of God. The axe strikes, and strikes again, and the tree comes crashing to the ground. Its proud trunk lies prostrate; its flourishing foliage withers and dies; its branches are stripped and bare. The tables are turned on Nebuchadnezzar. In the past he himself had wielded the axe as, for example, in his attack on Tyre, concerning which it is said: 'He will direct the shock of his battering rams against your walls, and with his axes he will break down your towers' (Ezek. 26:9). But now the axe is in another's hand and the judgment of God is about to fall on Nebuchadnezzar as it had done on the king of Tyre and for the same reason. Had not the king of Tyre declared, 'I am a god, I sit in the seat of the gods'? For this reason he would be 'thrust down into the Pit' where he would die 'the death of the slain' (Ezek. 29:2*ff*). And had not the king of Babylon said, 'I will ascend to heaven; above the stars of God I will set my throne on high'? And for this reason he too would be laid low as with an axe and be brought down to Sheol (Isa. 14:4*ff*). Likewise it will be with the self-styled Antiochus Epiphanes — '(God) Manifest'. Let him and all like him take warning; the axe has indeed been laid to the root of the tree.

In generation after generation God sends forth his watchers to declare his word of warning and of judgment, not only to nations and their rulers, but to all who fall short of his demands. John the Baptist was one of these. He made no attempt to lighten the blow which was about to fall on the Pharisees and Sadducees of his day: 'Even now the axe is laid to the root of the trees; every tree therefore that does not bear good fruit is cut down and thrown into the fire' (Matt. 3:10). The reason for this drastic action may be lack of fruit as in the case of the Pharisees and Sadducees, or overweening pride as in the case of Nebuchadnezzar; but, for whatever reason, the judgment of God is something to be reckoned with. In Old Testament and New Testament alike the thud of the axe can be clearly heard, as can the crash of the trees themselves, as God's judgment falls first on one and then on another. The 'Day of the Lord' in Amos and the 'Wrath of God' in Paul are deeply embedded in the teaching of both Judaism and Christianity. The sound of judgment rings out loud and clear against all kinds of evil, and not least against that pride which thinks of itself more highly than it ought to think (*cf* Rom. 12:3), or imagines that it is God (*cf* Gen. 3:5; 11:3*ff*).

Sometimes the judgment is self-inflicted; but for that reason it may be no less a judgment of God. How many of the judgments that fall on our society and our civilisation are the result of our own pride or greed or lust. The tragedy is, moreover, not only that we ourselves are brought low, but that, like felled trees in a forest, we so readily pull others down with us, forcing them to suffer a fate they did not rightly deserve.

The judgment meted out to Nebuchadnezzar in his dream was a dire one indeed. But it was not untouched by mercy for, though the tree is cut down, its stump remains, firmly held together with a band of iron and bronze (Dan. 4:15). He himself will come under severe judgment, but his kingdom will not be utterly destroyed. Then quite suddenly the metaphor of the tree is dropped and 'it' (the stump) becomes 'he' (the king) who will be 'wet with the dew of heaven' and 'his lot [will] be with the beasts in the grass of the earth' (Dan. 4:15). The king loses his reason and a 'beast's mind [is] given to him [until] seven times (presumably seven years) pass over him' (Dan. 4:16). This is done that he may know that the Most High is indeed the sovereign Lord 'who rules the kingdom of men, and gives it to whom he will' (Dan. 4:25).

5 A mad monarch

Nebuchadnezzar is afflicted with a disease in which the sufferer believes himself to be an animal and begins to behave like one. In his case the animal is an ox; he is 'made to eat grass ... [and is] wet with the dew of heaven' (Dan. 4:25). Instead of enjoying civilised society, he is 'driven from among men'; instead of eating at table, he 'ate grass like an ox'; instead of tidy appearance 'his hair [is] as long as eagles' feathers'; instead of manicured fingers 'his nails [are] like birds' claws' (Dan. 4:33). There is no independent record of Nebuchadnezzar having been afflicted in this way and it may be that the name of another king, Nabonidus, of whom it is recorded 'the king is mad', appeared in the original tradition. Be that as it may, the first readers of the Book of Daniel would again see a clear parallel in the king of their own time whom they nicknamed, not Antiochus Epiphanes ('God Manifest'), but Antiochus Epimanes (the Madman), whose behaviour ranged from the antics of the clown to the cruelty of the beast.

Sadly, history has produced not a few like Nebuchadnezzar and Antiochus whose madness has run amock and whose megalomania has resulted in untold misery. Whenever a man, be he ruler or not, aspires to become God, he ceases to be even a man and becomes an animal. Claiming for himself divine status, he forfeits his human status as one made in the image of God and is reduced to the level of the beast.

6 A call to repentance

Daniel is dismayed at the thought of having to tell the king the interpretation of the dream 'and his thoughts alarmed him' (Dan. 4:19). It is often difficult, when confronted by tyranny or oppression, to know how to respond. Should it be with discretion or should it be with valour? Should it be with confidence-building measures or should it be with confrontation? What price will have to be paid, not just by the person involved, but by the whole community he represents? How will it affect present witness and future action? In such circumstances we have to be 'wise as serpents' and not just 'innocent as doves' (Matt. 10:16).

Daniel is careful; but he does not shirk the issue. As unerringly as Nathan to David, (*cf* II Sam. 12:7), he points the finger straight at Nebuchadnezzar: 'It is you, O king, who have grown and become strong' (Dan. 4:22). Then, having given the dream's interpretation of judgment, he strikes while the iron is hot: 'Therefore, O king, let my counsel be acceptable to you; break off your sins by practising righteousness, and your iniquities by showing mercy to the oppressed' (Dan. 4:27). Let the king redeem the situation by acting justly towards his people and by showing mercy to those who are downtrodden. Repentance is not just a change of mind, it is at the same time a change of direction; it is not simply an act of confession addressed to God, it is at the same time an act of reparation addressed to those we have wronged. Daniel makes this clear to the king. But sadly there is no sudden conversion. At the end of twelve months the threatened judgment has not occurred (Dan. 4:29). The axe has not cut into the trunk of the tree; it stands as tall and as proud as it has ever been. 'Is not this great Babylon, which I have built by my mighty power ... for the glory of my majesty?' (Dan. 4:30). The passing of time and deferment of judgment have made Nebuchadnezzar over-complacent. His pride is stronger than ever. He struts like a peacock 'on the roof of the royal palace' (Dan. 4:29).

But still God is patient with him. A warning has been given by the watcher; now it comes a second time in a voice from heaven itself (Dan. 4:31). It is not God's will that 'any should perish, but that all should reach repentance' (II Peter 3:9). He is forbearing, despite our pride, our stupidity, our stubbornness, our rebellion. As in the case of Jonah, he gives us a second chance (*cf* Jonah 3:1). As in the case of the thief on the cross, he gives time for repentance right up to the point of death itself (*cf* Luke 23:43).

7 Judgment falls

But for Nebuchadnezzar the time is short. No sooner has the voice from heaven spoken than the judgment falls: 'he was driven from among men, and ate grass like an ox' (Dan. 4:33). The mills of God grind slowly, but they grind exceedingly small. There is an inevitability about divine judgment that only the grace of God through repentance can turn aside. It is not mere retribution, for God does not will the death of any man. Unrepented sin carries with it its own dire penalty. But God is merciful, and through his kindness seeks to lead us to repentance (*cf* Rom. 2:4).

Sometimes the judgment falls on individuals and at other times on nations, for Nebuchadnezzar stands here not in his own right only, but also as the representative and ruler of his people. He and his empire are called to repentance, and he and his empire come under judgment. This being so, the Christian Church, like the watcher and the voice from heaven, has the solemn duty to call on both men and nations to renounce evil and to do good lest devastating judgment fall upon them. Such a prophetic voice was perhaps never more needed than it is now, for if the judgment incurred is commensurate with the sin committed, then our generation and our civilisation are under terrible judgment indeed. The warning has been given, not once but twice. Who can tell when the axe will be laid to the root of the tree?

8 Restoration

At the end of the seven times (Dan. 4:23,34), during which Nebuchadnezzar lives and behaves like a beast, two things happen to him: 'my reason returned to me, and I blessed the Most High, and praised and honoured him who lives for ever' (Dan. 4:34,36). First, his reason returns to him and he becomes a man again. It is in the will of God that we should be 'fully human'. To deprive our fellow man (as is so often the case in our modern world) of those qualities of dignity and freedom which give him worth as a human being is to deny his basic humanity and to reverse God's order of creation who, having created the animals each according to its own kind, made man in his own image (*cf* Gen. 1:24–26).

Second, he confesses his faith in the Most High God and recognises his kingdom as an everlasting kingdom (Dan. 4:34). It is surely significant that his restoration to humanness and his recognition of God should go together. When we honour God, we value our neighbour; and when we dishonour God, we devalue our neighbour. And the reverse is equally true — Nebuchadnezzar sees sense when he sees God.

And as he is given a second chance to repent, so he is given a second chance to reign: 'I was established in my kingdom' (Dan. 4:36). He has learned his lesson from bitter experience that 'those who walk in pride [God] is able to abase' (Dan. 4:37).

5

The Writing on the Wall

1 A great feast

Belshazzar, who served as regent for his father Nabonidus, is presented here as a king in succession to his 'father' Nebuchadnezzar. Such historical discrepancy in no way takes away from the story which is narrated by a consummate story-teller.

The setting is that of a great orgy, attended by everyone who really mattered in the kingdom of Babylon. Little did they know, as they took part in their carousels and drunken frolics, that the enemy was already at the gate and their mighty empire was about to fall. For the moment all was fun and games, with plenty of wine to oil the machinery. We know from other external sources that the Babylonians had a weakness for alcohol and that on this particular day in question the citizens drank and enjoyed themselves all night long. Well might they have benefited from the words of the Jewish sage Ben Sira when he wrote:

'Do not aim to be valiant over wine, for wine has destroyed many ... Wine drunk to excess is bitterness of soul, with provocation and stumbling. Drunkenness increases the anger of a fool to his injury, reducing his strength and adding wounds'.

(Ecclus. 31:25,29*f*)

And with wine went women. Some sources, like that of the Book of Daniel, say that these were the wives and concubines of the king and his lords (Dan. 5:3). Others say that they were the concubines only. Whatever may be the case, it was a night of revelry, with no inhibitions, in which drink inflamed and passions ran wild. In the words of Walter Lüthi, we have:

'a picture of the deepest moral depravity ... In this king's palace we get a glimpse of the world as it always is in the last stages before a cataclysm. Evil has overflowed its channels. All barriers are down. Sin has now got to the point where ripeness becomes rottenness. The merest trifle will start the headlong rush to ruin'.

(Op cit, p 71).

He likens it to the damp, sultry atmosphere that hung over Sodom and Gomorrah in the days of Lot, and over the Flood generation in the days of Noah when 'they were eating and drinking, marrying and giving in marriage ... until the Flood came and swept them all away' (Matt. 24:38*f; cf* Gen. 6:5 *ff*). Belshazzar, behind the alcoholic haze, must have had some inkling at least of the gravity of the occasion, as the subsequent story makes plain. But for the moment all was well, and so with boisterous brigado the carousels continued.

But a diversion was called for, and so Belshazzar 'commanded that the vessels of gold and of silver which Nebuchadnezzar his father had taken out of the Temple in Jerusalem be brought ... that [they] might drink from them' (Dan. 5:2). These words would be full of meaning to the first readers of the Book of Daniel in the time of Antiochus IV, for it was that monarch's chief official, Andronicus, who had removed several gold vessels from the Temple in their day: '[he] arrogantly entered the sanctuary and took ... the silver and the gold, and the costly vessels' (I Macc. 1:21 *ff*). This same ruler, like Belshazzar before him, showed total disregard for those things which his unwilling subjects held most dear: the Temple and its sacred vessels, the Torah and its sacred scrolls, the religious festivals, the dietary laws, the sacred altar and the Sabbath day.

And the mockery and misuse of sacred things has continued to this day: the confiscation of scrolls and Bibles, the desecration of synagogues and churches, the proscription of rites and customs, the denial of free assembly to practise the faith. The gold and silver vessels, dedicated to the service of God, have all too often been diverted to other use: synagogues have become cinemas, and churches museums; ikons have become 'decorations', and sacred writings 'works of art'.

That attitude of mind which is 'at enmity with God' must

try to justify itself, and this it does by discrediting what is holy, by desecrating what is sacred, by shaming what is innocent and by degrading what is of moral worth. God's sacred vessels are always vulnerable; they can be put to the basest use, removed in a moment from sacrament to saloon. But God is patient, and his people must be patient too. There is to be a day of reckoning when all such acts will be taken into account. Belshazzar's carousels were but the tortuous antics of a doomed man. His self-justification was in truth self-condemnation. In commanding that the sacred vessels be brought, he was announcing his own destruction.

Having quaffed the wine from the sacred goblets, Belshazzar and his guests, no doubt in their drunken stupor, praised the gods of gold and silver from which metals the goblets had been made. There were gods too of bronze, iron, wood and stone; but those of gold and silver were given pride of place. Among the 'sins' most strongly condemned by the Jews was that of idolatry which was a flagrant denial of the God-given command, 'You shall have no other gods before me' (Exod. 20:3). Such condemnation was just as strong in the second century BC when the Book was written as it had been in the time of Isaiah of Babylon: 'Those who lavish gold from the purse, and weigh out silver in the scales, hire a goldsmith, and he makes it into a god; then they fall down and worship' (Isa. 40:20). How can men worship gods that are chained to the wall lest they topple over and fall flat on their faces (*cf* Isa. 40:20), when they could be worshipping the great and living God?

It is a question that is every bit as relevant today. Gods of gold and silver are still worshipped by many in that High Temple of Finance, the Stock Exchange; others are propped up precariously in many a Board Room; and others again appear as humble household gods. Their devotees are dedicated people, swearing allegiance to their gods even when their self-appointed deity lets them down. 'Their idols [of silver and gold]', says Jeremiah, 'are like scarecrows in a cucumber field, and they cannot speak ... neither is it in them to do good' (Jer. 10:5). But Belshazzar and his guests knew no better; they drank their wine and praised their gods.

2   A mysterious hand

Then suddenly, in the midst of the revelry, a mysterious hand appeared out of nowhere and began to write 'on the plaster of the wall ... and the king saw the hand as it wrote' (Dan. 5:5). He could not understand what it wrote. But he knew within himself that the hand was that of a divine messenger and that it conveyed a dire warning he dare not brush aside. His foreboding turned into terror: 'the king's colour changed, and his thoughts alarmed him; his limbs gave way, and his knees knocked together' (Dan. 5:6). The apparition might have been the result of a drunken hallucination or of a guilty conscience; but to Belshazzar it was a hand of divine retribution. He had before him the example of his 'father', Nebuchadnezzar, who had repented and been restored. And here was the same God giving him the chance to do the same thing. He did not know the meaning of the message written on the wall, but he sensed that time was short and that he stood in a moment of great danger for himself and for his empire.

In every moment of crisis such a hand appears and writes clearly on the wall. Our own day is no exception. We may not be able, from where we stand, to interpret fully the message. But we know only too well its purport. We know for a certainty that, if the warning is not heeded, our time is short. The hand of the nuclear clock has long passed the eleventh hour and stands now at one minute to midnight. Says a recent writer:

'From the dawn of consciousness, until 6 August 1945 (when the first atomic bomb was dropped on Hiroshima), man has had to live with the prospect of his death as an individual; since that day he has had to live with the prospect of his extinction as a species.'

(Arthur Koestler, quoted by Jim Garrison, *The Darkness of God: Theology after Hiroshima*, 1982, p 69)

But still there is time — just. The clock still ticks on and every second counts. We too have cause to be afraid. We may not be versed in the laws of nuclear physics; but we at least have had the example of Chernobyl to call us to repentance with its devastation over the face of the whole globe, to last for many years. Our generation has been warned. The writing is clearly on the wall for all to see.

3 A perplexed king

But Belshazzar was in no mood to repent. Instead, he brazened it out, hoping perhaps that the interpretation of the writing would prove his forebodings wrong. To this end he called in the wise men of Babylon and offered them the inducements he was wont to give when seeking favours — guaranteed wealth and preferment in office: 'whoever reads this writing, and shows me its interpretation shall be clothed with purple, and have a chain of gold about his neck, and shall be the third ruler in the kingdom' (Dan. 5:7). But his bribes and blandishments were of no avail: 'they could not read the writing or make known to the king the interpretation' (Dan. 5:8) There is a mystery whose meaning money cannot buy, and there is a destiny beyond the reach of human wisdom.

Belshazzar's fears turned into terror and he was 'greatly alarmed ... and his lords were perplexed' (Dan. 5:9). They were perplexed not just because the king was alarmed, but because presumably they did not know the cause of his upset. For the king alone 'saw the hand as it wrote' (Dan 5:5). All that his lords and ladies saw was a plain, white, plaster wall. But Belshazzar saw it because, although it was a divine hand, it might have been his own. It was as if he was writing his own obituary and that of his empire, and in this moment of truth the devastating reality of the situation came home to him with frightening force. But there was nothing he could do about it — the die was cast.

The world is full of perplexed people. They know that something is wrong and catch the alarm that is in the air. The politicians and scientists are in a position to see more clearly than most others that there is writing on the wall. Some, perhaps, are too drunk (with power?) to see what it is really saying, and others are too blind to see any distance ahead. But in their heart of hearts they must see the warning, even if they do not as yet understand its full meaning. The hand may be God's hand, but the writing looks very familiar — it is remarkably like their own. They themselves have determined the destiny that is now 'writ large' before the eyes of the world. They have a duty to share with their perplexed people the dire consequences of their actions and to repent before it is too late. The people demand to know, for it is their fate and not just that of the king that is at stake.

4   A sign of hope

The inability of the wise men to interpret the writing added frustration to Belshazzar's fear. Matters had reached an impasse when, quite unexpectedly, the door of the banqueting chamber swung open and in stepped 'the queen', or rather the queen-mother, widow of Belshazzar's 'father' Nebuchadnezzar (Dan. 5:10). It is just possible that, with wine and women, his mother was the last person Belshazzar wanted to see at that moment. God has strange ways of dealing with us. Sometimes he frightens us, and sometimes he simply embarrasses us. No doubt Belshazzar was embarrassed. But he soon realised that his mother had come not to scold him, but to offer him hope: 'There is in your kingdom a man in whom is the spirit of the holy gods' (Dan. 5:11).

In the days of Nebuchadnezzar Daniel had shown that light and understanding which could come only from God (*cf* Dan. 2:22) and demonstrated a wisdom which was 'like the wisdom of the gods' themselves (Dan. 5:11). His ability to penetrate the dark mysteries of 'dreams', 'riddles' and 'problems' (Dan. 5:12), was a gift from God and not just some innate quality or native intelligence which gave him a greater IQ than anyone else. It was something given him from above for which he himself could claim no credit. 'The spirit of wisdom' is 'the spirit of God'.

And yet it is inseparable from the spirit of man: the spirit of the holy gods is equated with 'an excellent spirit, knowledge and understanding' to be found in Daniel himself (Dan. 5:12). Divine revelation is hardly distinguishable from spiritual insight, and the voice of God from moral consciousness. This seems to be implied elsewhere in the Old Testament also, as in Proverbs 20:27: 'The spirit of man is the lamp of the Lord, searching all his innermost parts'. And yet they are not altogether identical: wisdom, knowledge and understanding are not simply the fruit of man's genius, but are given primarily by God's inspiration. As Elihu says in the Book of Job: 'It is the spirit in a man, the breath of the Almighty, that makes him understand. It is not the old that are wise, nor the aged that understand what is right' (Job 32:8*f*).

Wisdom may indwell a man and belong to him; genius may mark him out from his fellows as someone quite different or superior. But such qualities are in the final analysis 'given'; they have their origin in God and not simply in human nature. And as with natural gifts, so also with the spiritual gifts of salvation and acceptance with God: 'By grace you have been saved through faith; and this is not your own doing, it is the gift of God — not because of works, lest any man should boast' (Eph. 2:8*f*). Daniel, a man of knowledge and understanding, was one in whom dwelt the wisdom of the gods (Dan. 5:11).

Daniel had already acknowledged in the presence of Belshazzar's 'father' Nebuchadnezzar that the source of his wisdom was to be found not in himself but in the God who reveals mysteries (*cf* Dan. 2:28). But this did not prevent Belshazzar from pandering to such vanity as he might have had: 'I have heard of you that the spirit of the holy gods is in you, and that light and understanding and excellent wisdom are found in you' (Dan. 5:14). And to flatteries he added favours: 'purple ... a chain of gold ... the third ruler in the kingdom' (Dan. 5:16). But Daniel had no wish to appear in the king's Honours List: 'Let your gifts be for yourself, and give your rewards to another' (Dan. 5:17).

It is a temptation which the man of God and the Church of God must go on resisting. In an attempt to divert the word of God or to blunt his message of judgment, Belshazzar still uses flattery and favour, blandishment and bribe. He speaks condescendingly and ingratiatingly, heaping compliments on the heads of the exiles of Judah (Dan. 5:13) whom he really despises in his heart. He recognises their place in society, (limited though it may be), and offers them privileges they have not enjoyed before. He makes them feel important and offers them high office in Church or State. But God's word, which 'shatters the rock in pieces' (*cf* Jer. 23:29) will not be turned aside. And God's man, if he is like Daniel, will not be deceived: 'give your rewards to another' (Dan. 5:17).

And so Daniel confronts Belshazzar: 'I will read the writing to the king and make known to him the interpretation' (Dan. 5:17). But before doing so he reminds him of his 'father' Nebuchadnezzar. It was God who had given him 'kingship and greatness and glory and majesty' (Dan. 5:18) so that 'all peoples, nations and languages trembled and feared before him' (Dan. 5:19).

But by reason of his pride he was 'deposed ... and driven from among men' (Dan. 5:20*f*). But in spite of this clear warning Belshazzar had pursued the same path, desecrating God's holy vessels and worshipping gods of silver and gold, failing to honour that 'God in whose hand is your breath, and whose are all your ways' (Dan. 5:23). Belshazzar, like Nebuchadnezzar before him, was a powerful ruler. But he had overstepped the mark and there was no sign of repentance. The moment had arrived for judgment.

There comes a time, in generation after generation, when Daniel must confront Belshazzar and speak plainly to him in the name of God, however unpopular and unwelcome his word may be. The history books and contemporary records are full of such confrontations. One of these may be quoted here if only because it concerns the first publication in England of a plea for full religious freedom. It appears in *A Short Declaration of the Mystery of Iniquity* by the Baptist pioneer Thomas Helwys in 1612. Addressing the reigning monarch he says this:

> 'Our Lord the king is but an earthly king, and he hath no authority as a king but in earthly causes ... Men's religion to God is betwixt God and themselves; the king shall not answer for it, neither may the king be judged between God and man. Let them be heretics, Turks, Jews or whatsoever, it appertains not to the earthly power to punish them in the least measure'.

Thomas Helwys, unlike Daniel, was rewarded with imprisonment, disappearance and death. Alongside this we may set these words of Archbishop Tutu addressed to a prominent South African leader in our own time:

'Mr Minister, you are not God. You are merely a man. And one day your name will only be a faint scribble on the pages of history while the name of Jesus Christ, the Lord of the Church, lives for ever.'

Mercifully Desmond Tutu is still with us.

5 Weighed in the balance

At last the moment comes for the writing to be revealed and its interpretation to be given: 'And this is the writing that was inscribed; MENE, MENE, TEKEL and PARSIN' (Dan. 5:25). It has been suggested that these represent three weights or coins of different values — a *mina*, a *shekel* (one sixtieth of a mina) and two half *minas* — and that these in turn represent kings or kingdoms: Nebuchadnezzar, Belshazzar and the Medio-Persian empire. But, more important than the identification of the words is their interpretation. This is based on a pun in which each of the nouns signifying the weights or coins is pronounced as a verb so as to read 'numbered' (instead of a *mina*), 'weighed' (instead of a *shekel* or a *tekel*) and 'divided' (instead of a *half-mina*). Hence: 'MENE, God has numbered the days of your kingdom and brought it to an end; TEKEL, you have been weighed in the balances and found wanting; PERES, your kingdom, is divided and given to the Medes and Persians' (Dan. 5:26–28).

Behind these verses lies the story of the fall of the once great and powerful empire of Babylon. It has been counted great in the eyes of the world; it carried great weight in politics and in war. But from the divine perspective it was counted as small fry indeed and as light as the chaff that is blown away in the wind or burned in the fire — its end is destruction. It is the story of many an empire before and since. The message is written large and clear on the wall of history. He who has eyes to see, let him see.

And so the account ends dramatically. Having lavished his favours on Daniel — perhaps as a final demonstration of bravado — 'that very night Belshazzar the Chaldean king was slain' (Dan. 5:30). We do not know how. Nor does it matter. Nemesis had struck. The inevitable had happened. God had spoken. Belshazzar was dead. In these poignant words we hear an echo of other words in another age addressed to a man who also worshipped gods of silver and gold: 'Fool! This night your soul is required of you' (Luke 12:20). The story of Belshazzar, like that of the rich man in the Gospels, is a constant reminder that the arrogant cannot stand in the presence of God and that those who worship gods of silver and gold will in the end receive their due reward: 'He has scattered the proud in the imagination of their hearts, he has put down the mighty from their thrones' (Luke 1:51*f*).

'Belshazzar ... was slain. And Darius the Mede received the kingdom' (Dan. 5:30).

6

In the Lions' Den

1 Envy and jealousy

The theme of the 'moral tale' told in this chapter is all too common. It is a story of envy and jealousy leading to unjust accusation and the suffering of the innocent. Its sequel, however, is less common — the miraculous intervention of God, resulting in the triumphant deliverance of the accused and the destruction of the accusers.

Daniel's obvious gifts had been readily recognised by Darius and had gained him speedy promotion in political office so that the king 'planned to set him over the whole kingdom' (Dan. 6:3). The other 'presidents and satraps', who had to give account to him of all their doings, 'sought to find a ground for complaint against Daniel' (Dan. 6:4).

A number of reasons may be suggested for their behaving in this way. One is quite simply the natural instinct of sinful human nature to envy other people their success. It is a sin against which the New Testament, for example, is strongly outspoken. It was out of envy, we are told, that Jesus was delivered up to death (cf Matt. 27:18), and that there was quarrelling among his followers so that Paul has to urge them to 'conduct [themselves] becomingly ... not in quarrelling and jealousy' (Rom. 13:13; cf I Peter 2:1). There is only one way to counteract such behaviour: they must pursue that love demonstrated so clearly by Jesus himself and described so graphically in I Corinthians 13.4ff: 'Love is patient; love is kind and envies no-one ... Love keeps no score of wrongs; does not gloat over other men's sins, but delights in the truth' (*New English Bible*).

A second reason for their envy may be found in the fact that Daniel was a foreigner in their midst: 'one of the exiles from Judah' (Dan. 6:13). There is an obvious parallel between this story and that of Joseph in the Book of Genesis. But it can be paralleled too in every society and in every generation. The foreigner in our midst is an 'incomer' who does not 'belong'; his customs are different; his accent is strange; his 'birthright' belongs elsewhere. Strangeness breeds suspicion, and suspicion breeds resentment, especially if the one concerned is in a more favoured position than we are ourselves. And quite often this strangeness is compounded by the fact that the colour of his skin is different from our own. Xenophobia and racialism are close bed-fellows and are the root cause of much envy, jealousy, suspicion and hate.

But Daniel was not just a foreigner, he was a Jewish foreigner. And in the eyes of many people in many lands the Jew to this day has remained a particular type of 'foreigner', even though he and his forebears may have been loyal citizens of their country for generations past. Antisemitism is a virulent form of xenophobia and an equally virulent form of racialism. The 'wandering Jew' is not just a figure of legend. He is a real person, hounded from pillar to post in generation after generation for no other reason than that he is a Jew — different and so to be treated with suspicion; poor and so to be despised; rich and so to be envied; powerful and so to be criticised. Sometimes such antisemitism is open and blatant and leads to holocaust; more often than not it is subtle and silent, corroding society and corrupting personal relationships.

A third reason for their envy is to be found in Daniel's religion. Having found no ground for complaint in Daniel in his handling of the affairs of state, they look for some pretext 'in connection with the law of his God' (Dan. 6:5). The first readers of this book would no doubt at this point exchange knowing glances, for they knew from experience what this kind of treatment meant. In their day Antiochus, having taken political measures against them, went on from there to attack them on the ground of their religion. Sacrifices, circumcision and the Sabbath were forbidden; copies of the Law were destroyed; swine's flesh was forced down their throats; sacrifices were required to be offered on idolatrous altars; and, to crown everything, an altar to the Olympian Zeus was erected on the sacred altar in Jerusalem with an image of that god, bearing the likeness of Antiochus himself (*cf* I Macc. 1:41*ff*).

Such pogroms against the Jews have been all too frequent throughout history and have left their vile mark most prominently on our own generation. And in almost every case, whatever the pretext put forward — social, political or racial — they have somehow been religiously motivated. Antisemitism is more than a social phenomenon; it is deeply religious at heart.

And as with the Jew so also with the Christian, religious faith and practice are a continuing cause of offence, not least in societies which denigrate religion or even attack it as 'an opiate of the people'. For this reason religious liberty must be jealously guarded among those basic human rights which are the inalienable possession of all mankind.

2 The law of the Medes and the Persians

The presidents and satraps then proceeded to put their envy and jealousy into action. They persuaded the king to sign a decree to the effect that 'whoever makes petition to any god or man for thirty days, except to you, O king, shall be cast into the den of lions' (Dan. 6:7). And so the document was signed 'according to the law of the Medes and the Persians, which cannot be revoked' (Dan. 6:8).

The courtiers again used the age-old device of flattery to have their way with the king: let him play the part of God and require from all his subjects their worship and their prayers. The temptation to assume the prerogatives of God was always present with rulers in the ancient east, as the claims of Antiochius himself made only too plain. And of course it is a continuing temptation to the powerful, and not only to kings, in every walk of life. Such temptation is particularly strong in our own scientifically creative age, with its amazing feats of engineering, its tremendous advance in methods of flying and broadcasting, its discovery of jet propulsion and atomic energy and its travel into outer space. Is there anything that man cannot do? In the beginning, it is said, God gave man dominion over the beasts of the field, the birds of the air and the fish of the sea and over the raw materials under the earth (*cf* Gen. 1:28). But dominion does not mean domination; and man will be held responsible for how he uses it and how he abuses it. The earth is still the Lord's (*cf* Ps. 24:1), and man is still his brother's keeper (*cf* Gen. 4:9). Our God is a 'jealous' God who will tolerate no other, be it a deified man or a deified state. He alone is God.

The king then, persuaded by his courtiers to assume the role of God, signs 'the law ... which cannot be revoked' (Dan. 6:8). Here we have a classic example of the eternal, binding law of God over against the immutable, irrevocable law of man: 'the law of the Medes and the Persians' (Dan. 6:8, 12). Daniel, representing the people of God, stands between the two and has to make his choice. He knows only too well how vulnerable his position is. But he does not hesitate for one moment. With resolution he goes straight to his house and there, in defiance of the royal decree, offers his prayers to God. The resolution of Daniel stands in sharp contrast to the irresolution of Darius who, realising he has been trapped into doing something he had not really wanted to do, tries in vain to find a way out: 'the king ... was much distressed, and set his mind to deliver Daniel' (Dan. 6:14). But it was to no avail. He was bound hand and foot by his own law which could not be broken (Dan. 6:15).

The history of both Judaism and Christianity has demonstrated again and again how true to life this picture is: the prisoner is the free man, and his gaoler is in chains. 'Stone walls do not a prison make, nor iron bars a cage'. Freedom is not dependent on purely physical circumstances. It is a state of soul, a repose of mind and, for the believer, an attitude of trust in the utter faithfulness of God. The prisoner in the isolation cell or the inmate of the concentration camp is often more free than his captors and displays a serenity that confounds his persecutors.

The powers-that-be have good cause to fear men like Daniel who, for conscience sake or because they are bound by a 'higher law', refuse to conform to the accepted or required standards of their society, for the free man — because he is free — is a challenge to 'the system' which demands his total obedience. As Aegisthus says in Jean-Paul Sartre's *The Flies*, 'A free man in a city acts like a plague-spot. He will infect my whole kingdom and bring my work to nothing', to which Zeus replies, 'Once freedom lights its beacon in a man's heart, the gods are powerless against him' (Quoted by André Lacocque, *The Book of Daniel*, 1979, p 112). It is hardly surprising that those who seek to live by the law of God are often regarded not only as a challenge but even as a menace to man-made laws which deny the law of the sovereign Lord.

3   A man of courage and of prayer

When Daniel knew that the document had been signed, he did not take evasive or defensive action. Instead he did some simple, but positive, things: he went to his house, he threw open the windows, he faced Jerusalem, he went down on his knees and he prayed three times a day to God, as he was accustomed to doing (Dan. 6:10).

He went to his house. He might have gone straight to the palace and pleaded with the king; he might have remonstrated with his critics and given vent to his anger; he might have prepared for the worst by putting his personal bodyguard on the alert; he might have cut his losses and fled while the going was good. But he did none of these things. Instead, he simply went to his house. There are times when retreat is the best form of advance, when 'the low profile' is more effective than 'the public stance', when peaceful withdrawal is more powerful than aggressive attack. Such action in such circumstances is not a sign of cowardice or of weakness; rather it is a sign of wisdom and of strength.

He threw open the windows. One thing he was not prepared to do — to 'play safe' and to 'toe the line' by making no petition to his God for the next 30 days. He could, of course, have closed the windows and drawn the curtains and prayed in secret. But that too he was not prepared to do. He would make no pretence of his faith in God. He would openly acknowledge him, come what may — and the more who knew, the better. And so he threw open the windows and drew back the curtains and looked his accusers in the face.

The history of the Church is full of such illustrations of men and women who have refused to compromise or conceal, even under threat of torture and death. We honour them as martyrs of the faith. But we must honour too those who have closed the windows and drawn the curtains and have prayed to God in secret or in the privacy of their own homes. In the New Testament Peter and John are honoured by reason of their boldness in proclaiming Christ (*cf* Acts 3); but so too is Nicodemus who came to Jesus 'by night' (*cf* John 3:2). The story 'of the Church in China during and following the Cultural Revolution is one of secret gatherings for worship behind closed doors or in the forests where no prying eyes could see. But it is no less a story of great courage and deep devotion, deserving of the highest honour.

He faced Jerusalem. As the Muslim today prays towards Mecca, so the Jew in the time of this book prayed towards Jerusalem and the sacred Temple there. This was no empty ritual, born of habit and with no real meaning. Jerusalem was more than a city; it was at the same time a symbol. It stood for a whole way of life that was totally different from that of other cities. It represented a long tradition rooted in God's choice of Israel and his faithfulness to the covenant he had made with them. It spoke too of the unity of the people of God, wherever they might be. And it symbolised their future hope in 'the new Jerusalem', 'the new heaven' and 'the new earth' yet to be.

The Christian shares that same hope and prays for the coming of that new Jerusalem. But as he prays he looks, not to a place but rather to a Person. Christ is the ground of his being and his very life (*cf* Phil. 1:21). Through him God has entered into a new covenant with his people, sealed by his blood (*cf* Matt. 26:28). By him his people find unity within their diversity. And in him is focussed their hope for the world to come.

He went down on his knees. Daniel is represented as a man of prayer. He found himself in a time of great crisis when his very life itself was threatened. But he refused to panic. Instead, he remained calm and unruffled and gave himself to prayer. He was able to adopt this attitude because it had become his established custom so to do: 'he gave thanks before his God, as he had done previously' (Dan. 6:10). His regular prayer life prepared him for the time of crisis and enabled him to face it with equanimity.

Panic-prayers are all too common, like those of the shipwrecked sailors in the opening scene of Shakespeare's play, *The Tempest*: 'All lost! To prayers, to prayers! All lost!' The man or woman who make their way regularly into the presence of God have no need to go rushing in with frenzied cries for help. They know from long experience that God hears and answers prayer and can deal with any kind of crisis. And so, like Daniel, they can offer thanksgiving even before they seek his help: '[he] gave thanks before his God' (Dan. 6:10).

He prayed three times a day. Daniel had formed a habit of praying at set times to his God. Such a habit can, of course, lead to mere formality so that prayer becomes a chore rather than a blessing. But this need not be so. A disciplined prayer life is a safeguard against laziness and neglect and encourages that 'practice of the presence of God' of which Brother Lawrence spoke and which is the very basis of Christian living.

It is significant that, in all probability, these three-times-daily prayers of Daniel corresponded to the three-times-daily sacrifices offered in the Jerusalem Temple in the name of the entire people of God. Daniel was far away from Jerusalem, in the Dispersion in Babylon; but by means of prayer he identified himself with the worshippers in Jerusalem and recognised his oneness with the whole people of Israel, wherever they might be. We are reminded of the prayer of Jesus concerning his Church, 'that they all may be one' (John 17:21). The unity of the Church is something given by God which Christ prayed will be appropriated by all his people and become a visible reality among them. It is not enough that we should pray, worship and witness in isolation, in the privacy of our own room — or nation or denomination. We must seek to identify ourselves with the whole people of God, offering our prayers as part of their sacrifice of praise.

4   A miraculous intervention

Daniel's informers are a despicable breed in every generation — out of envy or jealousy or greed they are ready to spy on their colleagues or even the members of their own households and report them to the authorities. These particular informers lost no time: they 'came thronging' (Dan. 6:11, RSV margin), eager to get the evidence they so desperately wanted. They got it and reported it to the king. Despicable they may have been; but they were ready with their own defence. They conveniently neglected to say that the plot that had been laid was theirs in the first place and instead went on to justify their action by saying they were simply carrying out orders 'from above': 'O king! Did you not sign an interdict ...?' (Dan. 6:12). Who were they to disobey the king, and who was the king to disobey the unalterable law of the land?

The same plea was made monotonouly at the Nuremburg trial when Nazi leaders faced an indictment of dastardly crimes against humanity — we were only obeying orders; we ourselves were not to blame. Such self-justification is a common human ploy, so transparently thin when seen in the light of divine judgment. The responsibility is ours — 'the buck stops here'.

But judgment need not be the last word. There was one man there whose uneasy conscience led him in the end to repentance — none other than the king himself: 'the king ... was much distressed' (Dan. 6:14). Even in the case of those who are without the law, says Paul, that law is 'written on their hearts, while their conscience also bears witness and their conflicting thoughts accuse or perhaps excuse them' (Rom. 2:15). That conscience is sometimes seared as with a hot iron (I Tim. 4:2); nevertheless it exists and may lead to repentance and the acceptance of forgiveness through the immeasurable grace of God.

But the troubled conscience by itself is not enough to avert evil. Darius, the conscience-stricken king, was (as we have seen) the prisoner of his own laws and so 'the king commanded, and Daniel was brought and cast into the den of lions' (Dan. 6:16). Later, in the time of the Emperor Domitian, the cry 'to the lions' was frequently heard. Martyrdom has been a mark of Christian witness from the very beginning until now. And as in the time of Daniel, so in the time of Antiochus, of the early Church and of today, there have been those who 'through faith conquered kingdoms, enforced justice, received promises, stopped the mouths of lions, quenched raging fire, escaped the edge of the sword, won strength out of weakness, became mighty in war, put foreign armies to flight' (Heb. 11:33*f*).

Not all, however, have escaped unscathed like Daniel (Dan. 6:23), either from the furnace or from the lions' den. But they have experienced a greater miracle still — the God in whom they trust has been with them even in the midst of the flames and among the ravenous beasts. God is to be found in the most unexpected places — in the prison cell, in the psychiatric ward, in the broken marriage, in the wrecked business, in the redundant job, in the inoperable illness, in the shattering bereavement. He is there with us in the pit itself, warding off the lions and shutting their mouths. He may appear as 'an angel' (Dan. 6:22), or a messenger or a friend or a stranger; but, in whatever guise, it is God himself who is with us: 'the living God ... [whose] kingdom shall never be destroyed' (Dan. 6.26).

The Apostle Peter reminds his readers, 'Your adversary the devil prowls around like a roaring lion, seeking someone to devour ... After you have suffered a little while, God ... will himself restore, establish, and strengthen you. To him be the dominion for ever and ever' (I Peter 5:8*ff*). 'I know your tribulation', says the Spirit to the Church in Smyrna, '... Do not fear what you are about to suffer ... Be faithful unto death, and I will give you the crown of life' (Rev. 2:9*ff*).

5   A premonition

It is perhaps not surprising that the early Christians saw in this story of Daniel's miraculous deliverance from death a pointer to the Passion and resurrection of their Saviour Christ. The parallels between the two are indeed quite remarkable. Like the presidents and satraps (Dan. 6:4), the chief priests and elders seek ways to take away his life (Matt. 26:59). Like Daniel's informers (Dan. 6:11), Judas is prepared to act as spy and betrays his Master to the authorities (Matt. 26:48). Like Darius the king (Dan. 6:14,18), Pilate's wife is greatly troubled in her sleep and seeks Jesus' release (Matt. 27:19). Like Daniel who is found blameless before God (Dan. 6:22), Jesus is declared innocent and no fault can be found in him (Luke 23:4). Like Daniel in the lions' den (Dan. 6:16),

Christ goes down into the Pit of death (Eph. 4:9). Like the angel which appears in the lions' den (Dan. 6:22), a heavenly messenger announces that Christ is risen (Matt. 28:6). Like the king who comes to the den at the break of day (Dan. 6:19), the women come to the tomb in the early dawn (Matt. 28:1). Like Darius who rejoices that Daniel is alive (Dan. 6:23), the women depart from the tomb 'with great joy' (Matt. 28:8). And like Daniel who lives to prosper during the reigns of Darius and Cyrus (Dan. 6:28), Christ rises to reign in his eternal kingdom (Rev. 11:15).

But for all these similarities, there are at the same time profound differences. Thus, whereas Daniel's accusers are brought and cast into the den of lions together with 'their children, and their wives' (Dan. 6:24), Jesus prays, 'Father, forgive them, for they know not what they do' (Luke 23:34); his followers are not to avenge themselves (Rom. 12:19), but to pray for their persecutors (Matt. 5:44), and to forgive those who have done them wrong (Matt. 6:12). Whereas Daniel is rescued from death (Dan. 6:23), Christ accepts death (Matt. 16:21). Whereas 'no kind of hurt' is found in Daniel 'because he had trusted in his God' (Dan. 6:23), Jesus in whom there is no sin (Heb. 4:15), suffers the agonies of crucifixion and forsakenness by God (Matt. 27:46). And whereas Daniel is delivered by an angel, Jesus resists the temptation to call down twelve legions of angels which are at his command (Matt. 26:53).

Similarities and dissimilarities both declare that one greater than Daniel is here. With greater conviction and greater assurance than Darius, the Christian is able to say concerning his God revealed in Christ: 'He delivers and rescues, he works signs and wonders in heaven and on earth, he who has saved Daniel from the power of the lions' (Dan. 6:27).

7

The Judgment of the Beasts

Now it is Daniel's turn to have a dream. And what a dream it is. A great sea, writhing and roaring in turmoil; four great beasts, the like of which appear only in nightmares; a judgment scene, with the eternal God seated on his throne; and a mysterious figure to whom is given the victory and the rule for ever. It is an awesome picture whose symbols and metaphors tell the story of God's struggle against the powers of evil and of his ultimate victory in which the redeemed of all the ages will share.

1   The great sea

In his dream Daniel beholds a 'great sea', whipped into a frenzy by 'the four winds of heaven' (Dan. 7:2). But this is no ordinary sea, however rough and however turbulent. It is the mysterious 'cosmic ocean' so familiar to the mythology of ancient peoples, the symbol of chaos and destruction that threatens to engulf the world. It is the same great sea that was there 'in the beginning', when the earth was 'without form and void' (Gen. 1:2). God the Creator wrested the world from its grasp and saved it from the power of chaos, giving it not only life but order too in all its ways.

And this is what he continues to do, to save the world from the destructive power of chaos which continually threatens to engulf it. He stills 'the roaring of the seas, the roaring of their waves' (Ps. 65:7). This too is the testimony of Jonah who is assured that, though the waves close in over his head, deliverance belongs to God (*cf* Jonah 2:5–9). And John, on the isle of Patmos, rejoices that, with the coming of 'a new heaven and a new earth', there is to be no more sea (Rev. 21:1): disorder gives way to order, and chaos to cohesion, the powers of destruction are themselves destroyed and God's will remains supreme. It is this same confidence that Paul expresses, though in different language, when he cries, 'I am sure that ... neither height, nor depth, nor anything else in all creation, will be able to separate us from the love of God in Christ Jesus our Lord' (Rom. 8:38*f*).

God the Creator, who made heaven and earth and all that is in them, is also God the Redeemer who, in the beginning, saved the world from the power of chaos and in Christ redeemed mankind. It is just here that the doctrine of creation is so closely bound up with the doctrine of the incarnation, for in Jesus we know the Creator as he really is: in him we know that God's purpose in creation is one of ultimate redemption. By what he said and did, and above all by what he was, he came to show that God the Creator is indeed God the Saviour. In Jesus we discover the meaning of God's work of creation, for it pleased God 'through him to reconcile all things to himself ... making peace by the blood of his cross' (Col. 1:20). We know God supremely as Creator because we know him as Redeemer in Jesus Christ our Lord.

2   The great beasts

In Daniel's dream 'four great beasts come up out of the sea, different from one another' (Dan. 7:3). Both here and elsewhere in the Bible the forces of chaos, anarchy and destruction are represented not only by the sea but also by great monsters that dwell in the sea. In common with the mythology of other ancient peoples, the Bible gives them names such as Rahab, Leviathan and the Serpent, enemies of God, in constant conflict with the Creator. And just as the Creator is able to subdue the great sea, bringing order out of confusion, so he is able to destroy the great monsters, bringing good out of evil. Job describes the conflict in these words: 'By his power he stilled the sea; by his understanding he smote Rahab. By his wind the heavens were made fair; his hand pierced the fleeing serpent' (Job 26:12*f*; *cf* Ps. 74:13*f*).

Elsewhere in the Bible the imagery is transferred from the work of creation to the plain of history and in particular to two great events in the life of the Hebrew people, the exodus from Egypt and the return from exile in Babylon: 'Was it not thou who didst cut Rahab in pieces, that didst pierce the dragon? Was it not thou that didst dry up the sea, the waters of the great deep; that didst make the depths of the sea a way for the redeemed to pass over? And the ransomed of the Lord shall return, and come to Zion with singing' (Isa. 59:1*ff*).

In yet another oracle the conflict between God and the primeval monsters is projected still further, from history into the future, and becomes a sign of the End-time when God will subject all things to himself: 'In that day the Lord with his hard and great and strong sword will punish Leviathan the fleeing serpent ... and he will slay the serpent that is in the sea' (Isa. 27:1).

The struggle that began at creation and has continued throughout history will reach its conclusion at the consummation of all things. Chaos will be put to flight; confusion will be confounded; evil will be destroyed. The one who in the beginning created all things, and throughout history has sustained his people, will in the end appear as the mighty Saviour. God the Creator, who is God the Saviour, will bring all things to their completion.

This is the assurance Daniel is given in his vision. The 'four great beasts', he is told, 'are four kings who shall arise out of the earth' (Dan. 7:17). They in turn represent four kingdoms which are no doubt to be identified with Babylon ('like a lion', Dan. 7:4), Media ('like a bear', Dan. 7:5), Persia ('like a leopard', Dan. 7:6) and Greece ('different from all the beasts', Dan. 7:7). Attention is focussed on this fourth beast and in particular on a 'little horn' which emerges from it in which are 'eyes like the eyes of a man, and a mouth speaking great things' (Dan. 7:8). This is surely Antiochus himself who, though a mere man, speaks with loud-mouthed arrogance and behaves as if he were a god. In him evil is incarnate and chaos claims control. But, as at the beginning so too at the end, 'the beast was slain, and its body destroyed' (Dan. 7:11). 'The End' will be as 'the Beginning', when God created the world from chaos, and is the guarantee of 'the here and now'. The great Creator, who in the end will bring all things to completion, is with his people now in the struggle against evil and will give them the victory over all their foes.

This is the faith of the Gospel of him who overcame the powers of darkness and death and rose again triumphant. It is the faith too of his Church which lives and bears its witness on the resurrection-side of the cross. It refuses to give up hope even in face of the most fearful monsters that keep on rising from the troubled sea. This is the confidence of John, for example, on the isle of Patmos. He too sees a vision of 'a beast rising out of the sea' (Rev. 13:1*ff*), which shows all the marks of Daniel's four terrifying monsters. To him this beast finds expression in the Roman empire, and in particular in its emperor, who persecuted the saints and set himself up against the Lord's Messiah. In different generations it assumes different forms and is called by different names. In the nineteenth century one of its manifestations was called slavery which held thousands upon thousands of men and women in thrall. It was recognised for what it was on the island of Jamaica, for example: there, on the day of liberation on the stroke of midnight a coffin containing chains and shackles was lowered into a grave and the cry went up, 'the monster is dead!'. Today it assumes other forms no less frightening and is called by other names no less terrible. In South Africa it is the monster of racism called 'apartheid', which is indeed 'terrible and dreadful and exceedingly strong' (Dan. 7:7). In Europe and beyond it is the monster of militarism, that has 'great iron teeth' (Dan. 7:7). Elsewhere it is the monster of totalitarianism, that 'devoured and broke in pieces' (Dan. 7:7). And elsewhere it is the monster of materialism, that spawns cupidity and misery and 'stamped the residue with its feet' (Dan. 7:7).

One by one they emerge from the turbulent sea with threatening roars, terrifying all mankind. But as they emerge they are slain; or if perchance 'their lives were prolonged for a season and a time' (Dan. 7:12) — their doom is writ. The lion, the bear, the leopard and the fourth ferocious beast may boast their strength and claim their victims, but the ultimate victory remains with 'the Lamb that was slain' (Rev. 13:8) who alone is 'worthy to receive glory and honour and power' (Rev. 4:11), to whom is 'glory and dominion for ever and ever' (Rev. 1:6).

These 'beasts' are terrifying enough in themselves. Yet it

has to be recognised that they are but manifestations of an evil power which cannot be explained simply in human terms or be dealt with simply by human means. Later on in the book, Daniel makes clear that behind and beyond the earthly struggle, there goes on a corresponding struggle in the spiritual realm. It is his way of saying that the forces we struggle against are not just those of flesh and blood, but rather of 'the principalities, against the powers ... the world rulers of this present darkness, against the spiritual hosts of wickedness in the heavenly places' (Eph. 6:12). The struggle against the monsters is not just a social project or a humanitarian programme. It is a spiritual battle which cannot be won except by the power of God. In his name and in the power of prayer his Church must continue the struggle, knowing that victory belongs to our God (Rev. 15:2*ff*). 'Thanks be to God, who gives us the victory through our Lord Jesus Christ' (I Cor. 15:57).

3 The ancient of days

Quite suddenly the scene is changed and the reader finds himself in a heavenly court of justice. In the Judge's seat sits an 'ancient of days', God himself, flanked by his angelic counsellors. The figure of this Judge presents an awesome appearance, as frightening no doubt to the beasts as the beasts themselves were to Daniel. The whiteness of his 'raiment' and his 'hair' speaks of his absolute purity, and the 'fiery flames' and 'stream of fire' that issue from his throne declare his power to destroy evil (Dan. 7:9–10). The charge-books are opened and proceedings begin.

It is salutary to remember that the God whose name is love is the same God who will not tolerate evil and who sits in aweful judgment on the deeds of evil men. He is just and fair in all his dealings, but that does not make his judgments less awesome to those who flagrantly flout his laws. 'Shall not the Judge of all the earth do right?', asks Abraham as he pleads for the inhabitants of Sodom (Gen. 18:25). To Paul too he is the righteous judge (II Tim. 4:8). For this very reason 'it is a fearful thing to fall into the hands of the living God' (Heb. 10:31). This is not vindictiveness. It is not even strict justice. It is an expression of that love for the world that will not let evil have its way, but will always take the side of the oppressed, the rejected and the persecuted and save them from their distress. Speaking of his coming Passion and death on the cross, Jesus says, 'Now is the judgment of this world, now shall the ruler of this world be cast out' (John 12:31). The cross is at one and the same time the supreme revelation of God's love and God's judgment. These two are not contradictory; they are complementary in the providence and in the grace of God.

It is significant that the judgment-throne of God is set above the great sea and the terrifying monsters. As we look at them we are hypnotised by their aweful power. Their bestial deeds match their cruel demeanour. They claim to have divine control over the world and its affairs, arrogantly boasting that they have the powers of life and of death; and there are times when we almost believe them. They occupy our television screens, they fill our newspapers, they rear their heads in almost every news bulletin. What power can stand against them? Then we lift our eyes from the sea to the heavens and there we see a throne and on the throne the Judge of all the earth. We turn from the bad news of the bulletin to the Good News of the Bible and there we see what the unbeliever cannot see. We see a judgment-seat and on it one who will always uphold the good and condemn the evil, who will not forsake the innocent or leave them at the mercy of the beasts, who will rescue them and destroy evil from the face of the earth. Such a vision is given to the upward look of faith.

But there is a mystery here. The great beasts are destined to be slain, but in the case of the first three, though 'their dominion was taken away, their lives were prolonged for a season and a time' (Dan. 7:12), and in the case of the fourth, though it was indeed slain, its 'little horn' continued to 'wear out the saints' who were 'given into his hand for a time, two times and half a time' (Dan. 7:25). The mystery is to be found in this, that Almighty God allows the sea to rage and the monsters to trample the righteous underfoot. It is all the more difficult for the writer of the book to understand when he contemplates the situation in his own day and ponders the three and a half 'times' or years during which the tyrant Antiochus had suppressed Jerusalem and occupied the Temple there.

But the time will surely come when judgment will be given and the beasts will be slain. That time is in God's hands. It is not for the powers of evil to decide their own destiny. In his own inscrutable wisdom God gives them free rein for a while so that they may imagine they are masters of their own fate. But that is not so. There comes a time when God says, 'Stop!' And stop they must. The apparent triumph of evil over good will continue only so long as God permits. The trials of his people will continue, but God is still in control. This is the vision of that faith by which the Christian lives, a faith which is 'the assurance of things hoped for, the conviction of things not seen' (Heb. 11:1).

But the mystery remains. In the light of Christ's coming and in the light of Christ's cross, however, it is no longer a mystery of darkness; it is a mystery of light. We see our Saviour being delivered, not *from* death, but *through* death, and rising again in glorious resurrection. The mystery remains, but we know through him that we can trust our God even when gripped in the jaws of the beast. Even from there his throne is visible, and we can see that it is 'the throne of God and of the Lamb' (Rev. 22:3).

4   Saints and son of man

Judgment is given and the beast is slain. Then suddenly the scene changes again and on to the stage comes 'one like a son of man' who appears 'with the clouds of heaven' (Dan. 7:13). He is presented to 'the Ancient of Days' and, as in a royal investiture, receives from his hand a glorious 'kingdom' (Dan. 7:14).

The 'one like a son of man' presented here is not to be understood as the Messiah in this context. He is 'one like a mortal man' (for so the expression could be translated) who, in his very humanity, is to be contrasted with the beasts which have been judged or slain. The contrast is made all the greater when, like some divine being, he comes riding 'with the clouds of heaven'. To him God gives 'dominion and glory and kingdom' (Dan. 7:14). The sovereignty and power, once claimed and exercised by the beast, has now been transferred to 'the son of man' whom all nations will serve in a kingdom which shall not be destroyed (Dan. 7:14).

But who is this son of man? The key to his identification is to be found in Daniel, chapter 7, verse 27 where it is said that the kingdom, which in verse 14 is given to the 'son of man' himself, will be given to 'the people of the saints' (literally, holy ones) of the Most High. He stands as representative of the people of God. And who are these people described as 'holy ones' who are to receive the kingdom? Frequently, in the literature of this period, the expression is used to describe the angels, and it has been suggested that the son of man figure here may represent the archangel Michael or Gabriel and that the saints are their angelic hosts. But the whole context of the vision and its interpretation indicates rather that they are those Jews who have been persecuted by reason of their religion, who will be vindicated and be given the authority claimed by the beasts. They are indeed 'on the side of the angels' in the sense that the struggle in which they are engaged is not simply against Antiochus Epiphanes, but against that power of evil in the world epitomised by that monarch.

Although within the context of this chapter the son of man does not represent the Messiah, in course of time he came to be recognised within a 'messianic' setting. The subsequent relationship between the two concepts is a complex one, not least within the New Testament itself. The indications are that Jesus, reading this passage with deep spiritual insight, recognised in the son of man a picture, as it were, of himself in his own messianic ministry and of his own role in the coming kingdom. The expression might have had for his contemporaries no messianic significance. But for him it was otherwise, for he too had been summoned by God to receive the kingdom which would have no end. But although he used the description 'son of man' of himself, he vested it with new meaning. Not only did he see it in terms of his own role as Messiah, he saw it too in terms of the 'Suffering Servant' of the Lord of Old Testament prophecy: 'And he began to teach them that the Son of Man must suffer many things, and be rejected by the elders and the chief priests and the scribes, and be killed, and after three days rise again' (Mark 8:31). Son of Man, Messiah, Suffering Servant found their single expression in him.

This Son of Man, together with the saints of all the ages, are to receive the kingdom from God the Father. 'Fear not, little flock', he says to his disciples, 'for it is your Father's good pleasure to give you the kingdom' (Luke 12:32). Meanwhile the struggle against evil goes on until the final victory is won. And the battle the saints are fighting, it is to be noted, is on the spiritual level (*cf* Eph. 6:12) and not merely the physical. It is that same power of evil against which Jesus fought and which he conquered on the cross. Through him the final victory is guaranteed, but the struggle goes on and has to be fought with resolution by all the saints.

They do not, however, fight alone for, like Elisha's servant of old, they see that the place is 'full of horses and chariots of fire round about' (II Kings 6:17). For those who fight 'the Lord's battle' against the powers of evil, so deeply entrenched in the world, there are unexpected and limitless resources made available which are heaven-sent and which are more than sufficient for us even in our most desperate need. 'My grace', says God, 'is sufficient for you, for my power is made perfect in weakness' (II Cor. 12:9). And again, 'From his fullness', says John concerning the incarnate Word, 'have we all received, grace upon grace' (John 1:16). Out of the unfailing and unfathomable resources at God's disposal we receive grace after grace — like one wave after another in the incoming tide.

Nor is it just the elite who are so favoured, as seems to be the case in Daniel's vision; God's grace and power are available to 'the very least of all the saints' (Eph. 3:8). 'The saints' are not a special class within the people of God, not a superior échelon. They *are* the people of God (*cf* Phil. 1:1). However lowly and however ordinary (*cf* I Cor. 1:26), they belong to the ranks of those whom God honours as his 'holy ones' and to whom, through Christ, he will give the kingdom.

5 The kingdom

In Daniel's vision the kingdom which the saints receive is seen in nationalistic terms. The faithful people of Israel, by God's help, will conquer the sinful nations round about so that 'all peoples, nations and languages' will serve them. They will set up a kingdom which will be the antithesis of the bestial and the beastly; it will be an earthly kingdom, but it will have 'everlasting dominion, which shall not pass away ... and shall not be destroyed' (Dan. 7:14).

There are those (Christians among them) who would see in these verses a reference to the modern state of Israel and its triumphant role in the fulfilment of ancient prophecy concerning the promised kingdom. But the whole notion surely runs contrary to the teaching of the New Testament which sees 'the new Israel', that is the Church, as heir to the kingdom. Like Daniel's kingdom it too is to be universal and everlasting, given by God and embracing a 'new humanity'. But there the likeness ends. The basis of Christ's kingdom is not one of race or nation, but rather of the response of faith to the God revealed in Jesus Christ his Son. It is not one of terrestrial ambition, but one of obedience to the message of the Gospel. It is not one of aggrandisement, but one of repentance, faith and obedient response to the will of God. It is a kingdom which breaks in with Christ's coming to earth, is operative now in the world like yeast in a barrel of meal, and will reach its consummation at the appearance of the returning Christ. The kingdom is incarnate in him, so that to be 'in Christ' is to be 'in the kingdom'. He is King and, together with his saints who are 'a holy nation, God's own people' (I Peter 2:9), will inherit the kingdom.

As such, they are to be a sign and an instrument of that kingdom. In bringing it, in their mission, by the power of the Spirit, is a continuation of the mission of their Lord himself: to preach the forgiveness of sins, to oppose the demonic powers of evil in the world, and to take the way of the cross. The kingdom of God is not just about 'the sweet by and by'; it is also about the here and now and concerns the lives of ordinary people on this earth. It is not just about the forgiveness of sins; it is also about the eradication of evil, in all its ramifications, from the life of the world. It is not just about my personal salvation or even the redemption of society; it is about the vast universe to which we belong and which Christ came to redeem — a cosmic redemption when all things will be brought into subjection to him (*cf* Phil. 2:11; Heb. 2:8). It is the kingdom of the Son of Man who lived and died and rose again and in expectation of whose return the Church continues to cry, *Maranatha*, 'Come, Lord Jesus' (Rev. 22:20).

8

The Ram and the He-goat

1 Horns

We read a great deal in this chapter, and elsewhere in Daniel, about horns. There is 'a ram [with] two horns ... one higher than the other'; there is 'a he-goat ... with a conspicuous horn between his eyes'; there are 'four conspicuous horns' which sprout up when the he-goat's single horn is broken; and there is 'a little horn' which in turn grows out of them (Dan. 8:3*ff*). The horn in the Old Testament is an apt symbol of strength and, within the context of war, a symbol of military might. The ram and the he-goat rely on it more than anything else. When confronting any rival they flaunt it and are not averse to using it. It is their ultimate defensive weapon and their chief instrument of attack. Their place within the herd depends upon it. They may snort and paw the ground; they may put on a show of strength, and rage at their adversaries. But if their horns are broken, they may as well withdraw whilst the going is good, for they are then an easy prey and will inevitably be gored to death. And so the more horns the better. Bigger horns and better horns spell salvation for themselves and the herd.

The same animal instinct is to be found in man. He glories in his horns. He claims that they are deterrents, to defend himself from the other members of the 'herd'; but he recognises that they can readily be used as offensive as well as defensive weapons. His opponents make the same claims and the same assertions, and soon they take up their defensive/offensive postures. They make ferocious noises in each other's direction and display their deadly weapons threateningly. They create more and more weapons, vying with each other and complaining that the other is taking unfair advantage.

They demand a balance of power, equal strength on either side and no secret weapons. They demand a careful examination of each other's 'horns' because they do not trust each other. They want to guarantee strict equality in the hope that this will lead to peace and not to 'mutually assured destruction' (MAD). This is no game of 'let's pretend'; or, if it is, it is the most deadly game that has ever been played in the history of mankind, for the weapons being displayed are potentially destructive, not just of 'the herd', but of the whole human race and indeed of the entire created world. That world will never be safe until the 'horns' are broken down and destroyed or until man's 'animal instinct' to fight and kill is completely transformed by the grace and power of God. Until the second of these is achieved, the first must be sought after night and day.

In Daniel's vision of the ram with its two horns and the he-goat with its single horn, the former, we are told, represents the Medes and the Persians, and the latter the Macedonian-Greek empire under Alexander the Great (Dan. 8:20f). The ram charges 'westward and northward and southward; no beast could stand before him ... he did as he pleased and magnified himself' (Dan. 8:4). A formidable foe indeed. Well armed and supremely confident, he is able to take on any challenger and demonstrates that fact by his very demeanour. So confident is he that he is able to entertain attacks from three directions at the same time. He feels — and knows — that he is the greatest. But ill-founded confidence, like pride itself, comes before a fall. Suddenly there appears a 'he-goat from the west across the face of the whole earth ... and the ram had no power to stand before him' (Dan. 8:5,7). So swiftly does he come that his feet do not seem to touch the ground (Dan. 8:5). And so fierce is his attack that he 'struck the ram and broke his two horns ... and trampled upon him' (Dan. 8:7). How are the mighty fallen. How foolish are those who trust in their proud 'horns' to deliver them: 'Woe to those who go down to Egypt for help and rely on horses, who trust in chariots because they are many and in horsemen because they are very strong, but do not look to the Holy One of Israel or consult the Lord!' (Isa. 31:1).

The he-goat feels he has good cause to be proud and so he

'magnified himself exceedingly' (Dan. 8:8). He has won a magnificent victory. But at the very moment of his greatest triumph, he finds that his own 'great horn was broken' (Dan. 8:8). He learns in that instant what nations and armies throughout history have learned to their great sorrow that in war, of whatever kind, there is no victor. War is self-defeating, and all are numbered among the vanquished. 'Put your sword back into its place', said Jesus to one of his disciples, who was prepared to defend him by force, 'for all who take the sword will perish by the sword' (Matt. 26:52).

The Hebrews found a better use for the horn than that of an instrument of war. The broken ram's horn, for example, was retrieved and made into an instrument of peace: as a trumpet it proclaimed the new moon, it announced the beginning of the Sabbath, it warned of approaching danger, it called the people to mourn the dead, it accompanied the healing of disease; and as a cup it was used to refresh one's thirst or to anoint a king with oil. In ancient art, moreover, the goat's horn has become a cornucopia, 'a horn of plenty', overflowing with flowers and fruit and corn. The instrument of destruction becomes an instrument of provision; the symbol of death becomes the symbol of life. The prophet Micah caught a vision of what things might be and what, one day, things will be: 'They shall beat their swords into ploughshares, and their spears into pruning hooks; nation shall not lift up sword against nation, neither shall they learn war any more' (Micah 4:3).

2   The ram and the he-goat

It is no accident that these particular animals are chosen to symbolise the Medo-Persian empire and the Macedonian-Greek empire. They in fact represent two signs of the Zodiac which in turn represent these two great world powers. In the Hellenistic age much attention was paid to the influence of the stars on human affairs and much use made of astrological symbols. According to the 'astrological geography' of the time the ram was represented by the constellation Aries which stood as guardian of (Medo-)Persia, and the goat was represented by Capricorn, the guardian of Greece. Such constellations, it was believed, controlled the destinies of men and of nations. The key to terrestrial history was to be found in celestial event. Wars on earth were determined by wars in heaven. Guardian angels were greater allies than neighbouring states. The calendar determined actions to be taken in war as in peace. Propitious times would bring propitious results.

Old superstitions die hard, and the signs of the Zodiac still rule. There are nations and rulers even today who, openly or otherwise, consult their horoscopes in the hope of finding the right time to take decisive action. So too with millions of ordinary people for whom their time of birth is of crucial importance, determining the sign of the Zodiac which in turn determines their destiny or even seals their fate. To most people astrology is an innocent pastime; but it reflects a deep-set hope in the human heart that beyond the plain of history and the course of ordinary events there exists a providence or a power that shapes our ends. For the Christian believer, that providence is to be found, not in the stars, but in him who 'stretches out the heavens like a curtain' (Isa. 40:22), and that power is to be found in him who 'takes up the isles like fine dust' and to whom the nations are 'like a drop from a bucket' (Isa. 40:15).

The two animals, then, describe in cryptic but dramatic form the rise and fall of two great empires. The Medo-Persian ram, with its two horns, was defeated in 333 BC at the battle of Issus and the coup de grace given two years later at the battle of Gaugamela. Alexander's conquests were swift and decisive, extending as far east as India: '[the] he-goat came from the west across the face of the whole earth, without touching the ground' (Dan. 8:5). But, alas for him, 'when he was strong, the great horn was broken' (Dan. 8:8). In 323 BC, at the young age of 33, he died and his place was taken by the Diadochi who ruled over his empire in four parts: 'there came up four conspicuous horns' (Dan. 8:8).

The writer of the Book of Daniel belonged to a small country which, again and again in the course of its history, had been crushed like a nut in a vice by the mighty empires that surrounded it. But he reflects that these successive empires, apparently invincible, had risen only to fall away and cease to be. Who would have thought that the mighty empire of Cyrus and his successors, or the even mightier empire of Alexander the Great would crumble into the dust of a bygone age? But that is just what happened.

Ancient history and the history of modern times together remind us that kingdoms and empires rise and fall, that kings and rulers come and go. Who would have thought, in the time of Queen Victoria, that the British empire, 'on which the sun never set', would cease to be, albeit by relinquishing its power? It is a salutary reminder to all great worldly powers that their span of life is limited and that their destiny is in the hands, not of the stars, but of the God of history before whom 'the nations are as nothing ... and as less than nothing and emptiness' (Isa. 40:17).

> 'Time, like an ever-rolling stream,
> bears all its sons away;
> they fly forgotten, as a dream
> dies at the close of day'.

3   The little horn

As in chapter 7 so here, 'a little horn' appears which 'grew exceedingly great' (Dan. 8:9). Once more the reference is to that arch-enemy, Antiochus IV Epiphanes. Not only does he grow great in the conquest of his foes, 'it grew great, even to the host of heaven; and some of the host of the stars it cast down to the ground, and trampled upon them' (Dan. 8:10). The same picture is given later on in the chapter in more prosaic language: there he is 'a king of bold countenance' who will 'destroy mighty men and the people of the saints' (Dan. 8:23*f*). God's saints are as 'the host of heaven'; to attack them is to attack heaven itself. This is made explicit in the verses that follow: not content with his attack on 'the heavenly host', 'the saints', he magnifies himself 'even up to the Prince of the host' (Dan. 8:11), 'the Prince of princes' (Dan. 8:25), God himself! Not content with political reprisals, he pillages the sanctuary (Dan. 8:11), and casts down the truth of God's word to the ground (Dan. 8:12). He is powerful, destructive, cunning, deceitful and arrogant (Dan. 8:24*f*). He is a villain and a trickster who tries to hoodwink even God himself (Dan. 8:25). He is self-confident, self-assertive and self-adulatory (Dan. 8:25). He is a great success in everything he does (Dan. 8:24) and prospers in every way (Dan. 8:25). 'But, by no human hand he shall be broken' (Dan. 8:25). The hand that cut the stone which smashed the great statue (Dan. 2:34), and the hand that wrote the judgment on the wall (Dan. 5.5), is the same hand that will break Antiochus in pieces who dared to set himself up as God. The lesson of earlier chapters is thus repeated and reinforced: the judgment of God is sure, and evil will be destroyed.

It is not surprising that Antiochus is regarded as the prototype of the Antichrist to whom reference is made in the New Testament (*cf* I John 2:18, *etc*), and elsewhere as the great enemy of the Messiah when he comes to set up his kingdom. Nor is it surprising that, in depicting the power of evil and the Prince of evil, medieval artists presented him in the form of a vile creature with horns in his head.

And yet it is all too easy to 'externalise' evil in this way and in so doing to excuse ourselves. We readily and rightly condemn the Antichrist, be he in the form of Antiochus of the second century BC, or the dictator, or dope-peddlar, or child-molester, or torturer of our own day. But it has to be confessed that we all share in that evil which is the legacy of Antichrist and which not only destroys men and women, but in so doing challenges even God himself. Some words of H H Rowley are worth quoting in this connection:

'The demonic Beliar stands for a persistent force of evil, not in any one man alone, but behind all evil men, incarnate in them in varying degrees. The human Antichrist stands, alas!, for the recurring Antichrists the world has seen. For the upsurge of sin in the human heart is fundamentally the same in all ages, and leads to the same sorts of character. The common sins that are in all our hearts, and all around us, are very much what they were in ancient days. And the rarer forms of sin in the overweening pride and ambition of men who attain power, but who lack humility, are also very much the same in the hearts of those who foster them. Hence, just as the lustful and the violent of one generation much resemble the lustful and

the violent of another, so the Antichrist of one generation
resembles the Antichrist of another, for he has the same spirit
of Beliar in him'.

(*The Relevance of Apocalyptic*, rev ed, 1963, p 174)

4   The end

The vision makes clear that, although the writer of Daniel
refers, albeit symbolically, to historical figures and historical
events, his real interest lies, not in the course of these events,
but rather in their culmination, when 'the end' will come and
God's Rule will begin. 'The vision', he is told, 'is for the time
of the end' (Dan. 8:17). That 'end', which will usher in the
kingdom, is bound up with contemporary event and the
overthrow of the tyrant Antiochus; and yet it signifies much
more than simply the end of his evil reign of terror — it is no
less than the end of history itself as men have come to know it
and the beginning of a new age in which God the Lord will
reign supreme. The kingdom which will appear will be an
earthly kingdom; and yet it is to be one with 'heavenly
overtones', reflecting those eternal values which belong to
that spiritual realm where God is.

Jesus, we recall, taught his disciples to pray, 'Thy kingdom
come ... on earth', and then added, 'as it is in heaven' (Matt.
6:10). That kingdom has to do with life on this earth, with its
secular involvements and mundane affairs; but it is to be
understood ultimately only in terms of the supramundane
and the eternal. It is at work within history, deeply concerned
with the events of history; and yet it is to be known truly for
what it is only at the end of history. It expresses itself in terms
of human endeavour and human love; and yet it is to find its
fulfilment, not in terms of human achievement but in terms
of divine gift. Its signs are to be seen in this temporal age; and
yet their realisation belongs to the eternal world where all
things will be brought to completion. It is present with us
now, influencing deeply the life of our society and our world;
and yet it is to be realised only in terms of its future
consummation. 'The kingdom here' and 'the kingdom there'
are ultimately not two but one. It will come 'at the end' with
the second advent of the Son of Man, but the beginning of

that 'end' is to be found in his first advent which is the guarantee of his second advent when all things will be brought to their conclusion by the will of God. In such a light we can see meaning in the events of this life and even in the sufferings endured by the people of God. In the setting of the kingdom, our lives and the life of our world are not only of temporal significance; they are of eternal worth and can become a sharing in the very sufferings of Christ (*cf* Phil. 3:10; Col. 1:24), through whose death and resurrection the kingdom comes 'with power' (Mark 9:1).

The writer of Daniel, then, believes that 'the end' is coming when God's Rule will be ushered in. But, more than that, he believes it is coming soon: 'For how long is the vision' (Dan. 8:13)? The answer he receives is positive and precise: 'For two thousand and three hundred evenings and mornings' (Dan. 8:14). The allusion is presumably to the 2300 evening and morning sacrifices, representing 1150 days which roughly correspond to the three and a half years towards the end of Antiochus's reign referred to in chapter 7 at the close of which 'the sanctuary shall be restored to its rightful state' (Dan. 8:14).

The sanctuary was indeed restored at that time. And yet the kingdom had not come. The great expectation voiced by the prophets had failed to be realised. But still the hope remained, and successive apocalyptic writers sought to re-interpret the oracles of the prophets and of Daniel himself in the light of the circumstances of their own day. And so it has continued down through the ages, not least in times of great persecution for the Church. Antichrists have been recognised in many evil contemporary rulers, from Nero to Hitler. Prognostications have pin-pointed the precise time and the exact nature of Christ's appearing and the advent of the kingdom. But still it is delayed.

We do well to remember the words of Jesus: 'It is not for you to know times or seasons which the Father has fixed by his own authority' (Acts 1:7). Such attempts to probe mysteries which belong to God alone do no honour to him or to the Son who came to reveal the Father. His assurance is enough, that in God's good time evil will be routed and the kingdom will come. And so the prayer of the Church continues unabated, 'Thy kingdom come ... Come, Lord Jesus'.

5   The vision and its aftermath

The vision and its interpretation came to Daniel as a divine revelation through the agency of an angel, none other than Gabriel himself (Dan. 8:16). Here, for the first time in scripture, a heavenly messenger is designated by name. These 'sons of God', as they are sometimes called, are messengers who convey to men messages from the Most High and play an increasingly important role in the thinking of early Judaism and in the New Testament itself. The writer of the Epistle to the Hebrews, among others, recognises their importance, but in the opening verses of his letter he points to one who is 'much superior to angels' and who, in his own person, 'reflects the glory of God and bears the very stamp of his nature' (Heb. 1:3*ff*). Supremely and uniquely, Jesus has shown a vision, not just of God's plans for the future, but also of God himself. Through 'his sufferings and subsequent glory' he has told us 'things into which the angels long to look', but which are hidden from their eyes (I Peter 1:10–13). He and he alone can make God truly known (*cf* John 1:18; Gal. 1:11*f*), so that he is able to say, as no angel ever could: 'He who has seen me has seen the Father' (John 14:9).

To return to Daniel, the effect of the vision and its interpretation on him was quite overwhelming: 'I was frightened and fell upon my face' (Dan. 8:17) ... 'I fell into a deep sleep with my face to the ground' (Dan. 8:18) ... 'I was overcome and lay sick for many days' (Dan. 8:27) ... 'I was appalled by the vision' (Dan. 8:27). He is overawed and overwhelmed by this divine encounter, for the archangel Gabriel is none other than a representative of God himself. In fear and trembling he prostrates himself before this divine majesty. The incident recalls another in the Gospels when Peter was confronted by his Master; so overwhelmed was he by the encounter that he fell down at Jesus' feet and cried, 'Depart from me, for I am a sinful man, O Lord' (Luke 5:8). He too was overcome by a sense of the 'numinous' — the awe-inspiring 'otherness' of Jesus — but it was an 'otherness' not so much of glory as of goodness. In the presence of his Lord he recognised as never before his own sinfulness and need of forgiveness. And yet, with nonchalance and careless ease, we so readily stroll into the presence of our holy Lord. Our only proper posture is surely prostration at his feet, and our only cry, 'My Lord and my God' (John 20:28).

But worship must lead to witness, and prostration must rise to active service: 'he touched me and set me on my feet' (Dan. 8:18) ... 'then I rose and went about the king's business' (Dan. 8:27). The touch is every bit as important as the spoken word: it expresses identification, it shows understanding, it conveys strength and power. Again and again in the Gospels we read 'and Jesus touched him ... and he was made whole'. The touch is itself part of the revelation: it heals the body, it soothes the mind, it restores relationships. And it sends us out on the King's business. It does not allow us to lie back in ecstasy, contemplating the heavenly vision; it sets us firmly on our feet and sends us boldly on our way. It points us down from the mountain top of revelation into the valley below, like the disciples from the Mount of Transfiguration to an encounter with an epileptic boy (*cf* Matt. 17:15).

Having explained to Daniel the meaning of what he has seen, the angel then bids him 'seal up the vision, for it pertains to many days hence' (Dan. 8:26). Its secret had been made known to Daniel by divine revelation, but even he has to confess, 'I did not understand it' (Dan. 8:27). Nor were things any different for the disciples of Jesus, for they too failed to understand what their Master was saying to them (*cf* Mark 4:13) or the meaning of the miracles he performed (*cf* John 13:7). But the time would come when everything would be made plain: 'What I am doing you do not know now, but afterward you will understand' (John 13:7). Meanwhile, says Paul, 'we walk by faith, not by sight' (II Cor. 5:7). With confidence, we put our lives into the hands of God in the assurance that in the end the mysteries of life — and of death — will at last be disclosed and we shall understand fully even as we ourselves have been fully understood (*cf* I Cor. 13:12).

9

How Long, O Lord?

1 The Books

Daniel is perplexed and longs for the captivity of his people to be brought to an end. Like so many of his compatriots, he keeps asking the question, Lord, how long? And in his quest he turns to the Books (Dan. 9:2), the sacred scriptures, and in particular to the prophecy of Jeremiah. There he reads the promise that God will restore Israel to its own land after a captivity of 70 years (*cf* Jer. 25:11–14, 29:10–14). But he is still perplexed, for Babylon has fallen and the 70 years have passed by. What can this mean? Is the prophecy mistaken, or is there some other explanation?

He is soon to find out. A messenger comes from God, none other than Gabriel himself, to explain the mystery. The 70 years, he is told, are to be interpreted as 'seventy weeks of years' (Dan. 9:24) which will bring the time of waiting conveniently down to the time of Antiochus and the writing of the Book of Daniel itself. The flickering hopes of the people are rekindled. The ancient prophecy is true — the day of deliverance is at hand. Jerusalem and its sanctuary, destroyed by Nebuchadnezzar and desecrated by Antiochus, will soon be restored.

Two important matters are highlighted in these opening verses which have remained central in the thinking of both Judaism and Christianity: the authority of the 'sacred Books' and the interpretation of ancient prophecy. The Books meant a great deal to our author. By the second century BC 'the Prophets', like 'the Law', had come to be recognised as a distinct corpus of literature carrying with it the authority of 'sacred Books'. Indeed, this is the first and only time the expression is used within the Hebrew Bible to signify 'the scriptures'. The full 'canon' of scripture, as it came to be recognised, had not yet emerged, but already the Law and the Prophets carried with them the authority of inspired writings through which the word of God could be heard. And in the pronouncement of Jeremiah, Daniel sees a prophecy of what is yet to be.

It has often been said that prophecy is 'forth-telling', not 'fore-telling'. But that is only partly true, for it does contain a predictive element and is concerned about the fulfilment or non-fulfilment of the words of the prophets (*cf* Zech. 1:6; Deut. 18:21; I Kings 22:1–28). But it is to be observed that:

> 'it was not so much in the foreseeing of the details of events that the predictive element lay as in the proclaiming of the divine rule over future history'.
> (A M Ramsey, *Peake's Commentary*, 1963, p 2).

This is true even of this prophecy of Jeremiah where the 70 years are probably meant to signify the span of a man's life (*cf* Ps. 90:10; Isa. 23:15) rather than a specific number of years at the close of which the exiles would return.

In due course the Christian Church took over these same scriptures (albeit in their Greek form), as their own and found in them forecastings of events yet to be which were to culminate in the person of Jesus Christ, the Son of God, in whom they recognised the fulfilment of scripture. These sacred Books, contained within the canon of scripture, are to be accepted as 'authoritative' in all matters of faith and doctrine, inspired as they are by God, treasured by the Church and illumined by the Holy Spirit. Such authority is to be found in their age-long witness to the character and purpose of God, as revealed in the story of his people Israel, culminating in the revelation of himself in Jesus Christ our Lord. Human words, albeit inspired by God, cannot hope to express adequately such a story and such a revelation, and the authority of scripture is not dependent on any theory of 'inerrancy' or 'verbal inspiration' or 'plenary inspiration' or even 'historical accuracy'. To the eye of faith it is the self-evident, self-authenticating word of God whose worth and authority are to be found in the revelation contained within these sacred Books.

But the opening verses of this chapter, together with their interpretation in verses 24*ff*, are of interest for another reason: they see the need to understand the scriptures in the light of contemporary event. This is a phenomenon which comes into prominence during the second century BC and is amply illustrated in the pseudepigraphical writings of the period as well as in the Dead Sea Scrolls. The form it takes is to see in ancient prophecy a hidden message, whose full meaning even the prophet himself did not understand, which is now made known to the seer whose responsibility it is to interpret it to his generation. In almost every case it contains a message relating to 'the end time' in which the interpreter believes he is now living. Thus, Jeremiah's prophecy of 70 years' captivity is interpreted, or re-interpreted, to signify 'seventy weeks of years' or 490 years which come to an end in the time of Antiochus which is the time of the writer himself. Such a word would come as a sign of hope to a people who had suffered much and could see no light at the end of the tunnel.

Interpretation of this kind can, of course, result, not in hope, but in further despair, if the time appointed arrives and still the promise of deliverance is not fulfilled. Nevertheless, the attempt continues to be made, and pious people juggle with figures, charts and diagrams, interpreting and re-interpreting Old Testament prophecies in the light of current events and in expectation of 'the end' which will not be long delayed. This is surely to mis-use prophecy which, as in the case of Jeremiah's words, is not primarily concerned about precise dates or 'allegorical arithmetic', but rather about the control of God over the events of history and his right and intention to exercise his sovereign rule through all the earth.

Altogether different from such mechanical manipulation of dates is the need to interpret scripture in such a way that it is seen to be apposite and relevant to the times in which we live. This affirms its original meaning and its significance within a given historical situation in biblical times, and at the same time it sees the same truth revealed, the same principles operative and the same God at work in our own day. In this way the scriptures do cast light on current events; they 'interpret' the news in our daily bulletins; they speak a powerful word to our generation; they carry with them the authority of divine pronouncement; they are the very 'word of God' to our generation. In every experience of 'captivity', in every time of crisis, in every moment of doubt we do well to turn to the Books in the belief that God has yet more light and truth to break forth from his word. The scriptures subscribe to no 'slide-rule theology' which plots the course of current events in the light of prophecy, nor do they foretell with precision the fast-approaching end. Rather they reveal a God who is in control, in whose hands are the destinies of men and of nations, and for whom the end will come when he and he alone decrees.

2 A prayer of confession

There is inserted at this point one of the most moving prayers in the whole of the Old Testament. It is a liturgical prayer as distinct from a prayer of private devotion and is a mosaic of biblical references, belonging probably to a much earlier time than that of the second century BC. But the Daniel of our story makes it his own as he contemplates the devastation of Jerusalem at the hands of Babylon, and the writer of the book makes it his own also as he contemplates the fate of the city and the nation at the hands of Antiochus. And we, his readers, make it our own as we contemplate the state of our cities and nations today and, as the Church of God, we make our confession of guilt and offer supplication that they may be spared a greater evil and the people may be set free.

It is a prayer for the city of Jerusalem (Dan. 9:16, 18–19), and the Temple within it (Dan. 9:17), that its people may be forgiven and spared (Dan. 9:18–19). The sins here attributed to it are the common property of all cities. They have done wrong and acted wickedly (Dan. 9:5, 8–9, 11): crime and corruption continue to flourish, and poverty and dereliction are all too common in the inner cities of our own land. They have not listened to the prophets (Dan. 9:6, 10): we too have failed to take warnings from the past or to learn from the mistakes of yesteryear. They have not repented and turned from their iniquities (Dan. 9:13): on the contrary we have sought to justify our actions on the grounds of expediency or partisan party politics. They have not entreated God (Dan. 9:13), or obeyed his voice (Dan. 9:14): and we have seen no need to bring religion into politics, but to confine it to the sanctuary (Dan. 9:17) or, at most, to special days of remembrance.

But Daniel makes clear that the city is very much God's concern, and for this very reason it must be his people's concern too. In the Gospels we read that Jesus wept over the city of Jerusalem (*cf* Luke 19:41). It matters to him, and must matter to his disciples, that in the modern city, young people are being hooked on drugs, non-whites are so often the object of discrimination, violence is rife, the weak are exploited, the poor become poorer and basic liberties are denied. God is to be worshipped in his sanctuary: but he is to be served also in the city where he himself lives and works — in its factories, its shops, its schools, its offices, indeed wherever men and women are met together in community. We are too quick to shut God up in church buildings or in religious ceremonies; he is to be found in the structures of society where he is to be worshipped and served. Religion is more than right ritual; it is also right relationships. It is more than religious observances; it is also right living. God is present in the proclamation of the kingdom; he is present too in the establishment of justice in the city. It is not without significance that John, in the Book of Revelation, sees the coming Rule of God in the form of a city, the 'new Jerusalem', where he will come to dwell among his people (*cf* Rev. 21:2; Heb. 11:10).

In this prayer of confession Daniel singles out 'our kings . . . our princes and our fathers' for special blame (Dan. 9:6,8). They hold positions of special responsibility in the land and so must be held culpable if, as they have done, they have not listened to 'the prophets, who spoke in [God's] name' (Dan. 9:6), and have sinned against him (Dan. 9:8). Statesmen and politicians and all others in positions of authority are answerable to the people for what they do or fail to do; but what they do not always recognise is that they are answerable also, and essentially, to God. And because so many of them, apparently, cannot or will not confess their sins of omission or commission before God, then the people of God must do this for them. 'I urge,' writes Paul to Timothy, 'that supplications, prayers, intercessions, and thanksgivings be made for all men, for kings and all who are in high positions' (I Tim. 2:1*ff*).

But Daniel's castigations are not confined to those in authority, culpable though they may be; they apply also to 'all the people of the land' (Dan. 9:6) to whose number he and his colleagues belong. Just as the sanctuary belongs to the city (Dan. 9:17), so the faithful remnant belongs to the people. Daniel does not stand over against the rest and say, '*They* have sinned'; rather he stands in the midst of them and says '*We* have sinned'. The people of God are not just part of the answer, they are also part of the problem. Repentance and confession are required of us, not only because of our attitude to God or to the people of God, but also because of our involvement in the sins and shortcomings of the society to which we belong and of which we form a vital part. It will not do for the Church to stand aloof in righteous indignation, giving the impression that it has no responsibility for the evils which afflict mankind today, except to condemn them as sinful and wrong. There is need for Christians to acknowledge not only their personal sins, but also their complicity and involvement in the corporate tragedies of their own day, and, with true repentance, confess their sins and those of their generation that, perchance, the world may be saved.

3   A prayer of supplication

The kind of prayer we offer shows the kind of God we believe in. So it is with this prayer of Daniel in his fervent supplication for the city of Jerusalem and for its people.

First, he is 'the great and terrible God, who keepest covenant and steadfast love' (Dan. 9:4). He is utterly loyal to the covenant he has made with his people, and his every action is motivated by love for them and for their wellbeing. There is nothing fickle about him; he can be trusted completely to keep his word, to remain true to the pledge he has made. Even a mother's love may at times falter (*cf* Isa. 49:15), but God's love will for ever remain constant. Even if we betray him and run after false gods, he will still draw us with 'cords of compassion' (Hosea 11:4), and never let us go. Such love is not just a characteristic of God; it is something that belongs to his very being. Indeed, it can truly be said of him that 'God is love' (I John 4:8). It is of his very nature to love us, despite all our failings and denials and sins, and to go on loving us to the very end. This steadfast love is revealed in many ways, but in none more than in the death of Jesus Christ, his only Son, our only Saviour: 'For God so loved the world that he gave his only Son' (John 3:16), and so 'we love, because he first loved us' (I John 4:19).

Second, he is the saving God: '[thou] didst bring thy people out of the land of Egypt with a mighty hand' (Dan. 9:15). Here is a miracle the people of God will never cease to wonder at. Out of all the peoples of the earth, God in his infinite goodness had chosen them. It was not because they were either great or good that he delivered them out of Egypt; it was because he loved them (*cf* Deut. 7:7*ff*). Sometimes he saves his people *from* their troubles; at other times he saves them *in* their troubles. Either way, he saves them. This too was the confident faith of those who came to follow Jesus in whom they saw the revelation of God the Father. 'You did not choose me,' he said to his disciples, 'but I chose you' (John 15:16). Like Israel of old they too were not among the wise or the mighty (*cf* I Cor. 1:26); they too would have to endure many trials (*cf* Matt. 10:21*ff*). But let them rejoice in their tribulation, for in course of time they, again like Israel, will obtain salvation (I Peter 1:9).

Third, he is a righteous God: 'he is righteous in all (his) works' (Dan. 9:7,14,16). This means more than that he will always do right and act with strict justice. It means rather that he will always act in conformity with his own character which shows itself supremely in steadfast love. As the righteous God, he is one who can be trusted through thick and thin, through fair weather and foul, when Jerusalem is prosperous and when its buildings and its walls lie in ruins, when things are going well and when life itself tumbles in.

Fourth, he is a God of judgment: 'he has confirmed his word ... by bringing upon us a great calamity' (Dan. 9:12). The prayer here reflects the theological outlook of the ancient Deuteronomic writers that calamity is due to sin: because they have broken the covenant, 'the curse and oath ... have been poured out upon [them]' (Dan. 9:11); they suffer a great calamity (Dan. 9:12, 14), and God's anger and wrath have made them a 'byword among all who are round about us' (Dan. 9:16).

Jesus saw both the truth and the danger contained in words like these. When asked if the 18 Galileans on whom the tower of Siloam fell were 'worse sinners than all the other Galileans, because they suffered thus?', he replied, 'No; but unless you repent you will all likewise perish' (Luke 13:2*f*). God does not act in an arbitrary or vindictive way; nevertheless, we continue in our sin and rebellion only at great peril to ourselves. The wrath of God (*cf* Rom. 9:22), is not to be dismissed as fiction, for 'it is a fearful thing to fall into the hands of the living God' (Heb. 10:31); but in his very judgment his mercy is greater than his wrath (*cf* Rom. 9:22*f*). There is a judgment of God in history and there is a judgment of God in the lives of individual men and women. It is true that we continue to reap what we have sowed, that acts of foolishness or sin may well lead to calamity, suffering or death. But this is altogether different from ascribing such things to a vengeful God who demands just retribution for all our wrong-doing. He who sits in judgment is the same God who loves us and will go on loving us to the very end.

Fifth, he is a merciful and forgiving God: 'to the Lord our God belong mercy and forgiveness' (Dan. 9:9); 'we do not present our supplications before thee on the ground of our righteousness, but on the ground of thy great mercy' (Dan. 9:18). These are great words, penetrating to the very heart of God himself and foreshadowing the confident faith of the New Testament scriptures: 'By grace you have been saved through faith; and this is not your own doing, it is the gift of God — not because of works, lest any man should boast' (Eph. 2:8). There have been times when this teaching concerning the 'free grace of God' has been forgotten and men have trusted in their own works and righteous deeds and have presented them as an oblation before God. But 'Christ has offered for all time a single sacrifice for sins' through which there is forgiveness (Heb. 10:12, 18). The prayer ends, then, not simply with a plea for deliverance but rather with a plea for forgiveness: 'O Lord, hear; O Lord, forgive; O Lord, give heed and act' (Dan. 9:19). Like the three-fold *Kyrie eleison* of the Christian Church, it pleads for mercy and forgiveness, and its prayer is answered by a merciful and forgiving God.

And *sixth*, he is a God who is quick to answer prayer: 'while I was speaking ... the man Gabriel ... came to me in swift flight' (Dan. 9:20*ff*). God does not wait until the prayer is completed before taking action. He anticipates his servant's supplication and sets about answering it with expedition: 'at the beginning of your supplications a word went forth, and I have come to tell it to you' (Dan. 9:23). 'Before they call I will answer, while they are yet speaking I will hear' (Isa. 65:24).

He is not a God who slumbers or sleeps (*cf* Ps. 121:3*f*); nor is he a God who is indifferent to our affairs (*cf* I Kings 18:26*ff*). He is one who is more ready to answer than we are to ask, more willing to give than we are to receive (*cf* Matt. 7:7*ff*).

Gabriel announces that he has come at once from God to give Daniel 'wisdom and understanding' (Dan. 9:22). Daniel's supplications will not change God's mind and make him do what he had not intended to do. Rather, they bring him a better understanding of the divine purpose and a greater appreciation of the divine ways. Prayer is not forcing the hand of an unwilling God; it is placing ourselves into these hands that we may better know his mind and purpose in order to do his will.

4   Seventy times seven

During the 200 years or so following the writing of the Book of Daniel many 'apocalyptic' books appeared, having as their theme 'the end' and the coming of the promised kingdom. The question on the tip of so many pens was, 'Lord, how long?' How long will it be before the people are delivered and the city restored? And in asking such a question they thought not just in terms of the Babylonian exile, but also in terms of their own 'captivity' under the oppressive rulers of their own day. They searched the scriptures for an answer and, as we have seen, concluded it was coming soon. Some went further and 'played the numbers game', indulging in a form of 'allegorical arithmetic' which made more precise the date of the coming kingdom. This chapter of Daniel is a case in point. The 70 years' captivity foretold by Jeremiah represent 70 'sabbatical years' (*ie* 490 years) at the close of which the people, like the slaves on the year of Jubilee, would be set free.

These things, says the writer, 'are decreed' (Dan. 9:26), and to prove the point he sets out the facts in tabulated form, beginning with the fall of Jerusalem in 587 BC as his base date and with the return in 539 BC: 'seven weeks' (Dan. 9:25, *ie* 49 years) from 587 to 539 BC. 'sixty-two weeks' (Dan. 9:25, *ie* 434 years) from 538 to 170 BC. 'one week' (Dan. 9:27, *ie* 7 years) from 170 to 164 BC, half of which remains (Dan. 9:27, *ie* 3½ years) from 167 to 164 BC.

His 'survey' of history and his references to recent events like the murder of the High Priest Onias III ('an anointed one shall be cut off', Dan. 9:26), and the setting up by Antiochus of a cult-image on the sacred altar in Jerusalem ('the wing of abominations', Dan. 9:27) — all this confirms the fact that God is in control and that 'the end is nigh'.

Jesus cautioned his disciples about indulging in speculations concerning the time of the end (*cf* Matt. 24:36), and urged them rather to read 'the signs of the times' with true spiritual discernment (*cf* Matt. 16:3). This he did himself, seeing in Daniel's 'wing of abominations', for example, a reflection of that 'desolating sacrilege' to which he refers in Mark 13:14 — an allusion maybe to the eagle ensign set up in his day by Pilate in the sacred Temple or perhaps a reference to the Antichrist himself who would appear to do battle against the Lord's Anointed. His disciples must be vigilant, watching for signs of the kingdom (*cf* Luke 12:35*ff*); but the time of its coming was not for them to know (*cf* Matt. 24:36).

But in spite of these warnings speculations and calculations have continued ever since. Not only times and seasons, but also people and places, have been identified in contemporary history, indicating not only the nearness of the end, but the means of its accomplishment as well. In our own day such prophecies and prognostications have gained popularity in many quarters. Prophecy and politics have mingled to provide a strange explosive mixture which can be highly dangerous when used in the propaganda machine. The political left and the political right have been positioned at different points on the spectrum of God's judgment according to the predilections of propagandist and preacher. Ancient prophecy has been torn up by the roots from the soil of biblical history and made to serve a purpose for which it was never intended.

One mark of the approaching end, to which reference is often made in ancient prophecy and in its modern 'interpretation', is that of war and destruction: 'there shall be war; desolations are decreed' (Dan. 9:26). Here it is described in terms of the struggle against Antiochus: 'the people of the prince who is to come shall destroy the city and the sanctuary' (Dan. 9:26). In the Book of Revelation it is described in terms of *Armageddon* (*cf* Rev. 16:16), when God's ultimate triumph will be assured over all the powers of wickedness. Modern 'spiritual speculators' have gone further and have claimed to identify the actual combatants in the fray. They are 'the capitalist west' versus 'the communist east', the United States of America (and Western Europe) versus the Soviet Union (and its satellites), the 'people of God' (the Israeli nation) versus the 'people of the land' (the Arab nations). Since the triumph of God is inevitable, the battle itself must be fought with courage and confidence; and so there are those who would prepare now for the war that is to end all wars, denouncing overtures of peace and decrying disarmament as contrary to the will of God. Such teaching is not only a denial of history and a perversion of scripture, it is at the same time a menace to humanity, for it has a habit of assuming the nature of self-fulfilling prophecy in which speculation becomes fact, and prognostication a terrifying reality. Such specious speculations and political propaganda are surely alien to the revealed word of God. The end, when it comes, will be safely in the hands of God, not ours. These things 'are decreed' (Dan. 9.26), and will come to pass in the way that he appoints.

10

A Divine Encounter

1   A revelation of the future

In the final three chapters Daniel receives a vision of 'what is to befall his people in the latter days' (Dan. 10:14). The content of the vision is given in chapter 11 and its conclusion in chapter 12. Here in chapter 10 Daniel is commissioned to be the recipient of it and is completely overwhelmed by the experience. He is given a hint in advance of what the vision is to be about: it concerns 'a great conflict' (Dan. 10:1), from which his people will emerge triumphant. In due course he will be able to say that 'he understood the word and had understanding of the vision' (Dan. 10:1). God's revelation would make all things plain.

The Book of Daniel is usually referred to as 'an apocalypse', 'a revelation' — literally 'an unveiling'. It is an uncovering of the mysteries of God in creation, in history and 'at the end'. The seer is highly privileged to be allowed to lift a corner of the curtain, as it were, and to see in advance what will be revealed to others only at the close of the age. Like a privileged guest at the unveiling of a statue, or painting, or plaque, he is given a preview of the finished work. All the other guests wait with eager anticipation to know what it is like. They have an inkling of what to expect and that has made them all the more excited. But he actually knows, for he has seen it for himself and is more than satisfied. He shares to the full their anticipation; he is every bit as excited as they are or even more so, because he knows for certain that what is to be unveiled goes far beyond what anyone could possibly imagine. Until now he has been sworn to secrecy; but the day of unveiling will reveal all. That day has at last arrived; only a few hours remain and then everything will be made plain.

111

Sometimes, as in this chapter, the revelation is described not in terms of an unveiling, but rather in terms of a book in which are written the things that are yet to be. The visionary is told to write down what he has seen and heard concerning the divine mysteries and to 'seal' the book (*cf* Dan. 12:4; Rev. 5:1, *etc*), until the last days when the seal will be broken and its contents made known (*cf* Rev. 5:9, *etc*). It is a transcript of what is already recorded in the heavenly places by the hand of God himself: 'I will tell you', says the angel to Daniel, 'what is inscribed in the book of truth' (Dan. 10:21). In the following chapter he fulfils that promise: 'and now I will show you the truth' (Dan. 11:1).

John, on the isle of Patmos, shares the high privilege enjoyed by Daniel. He too has seen 'beyond the veil'; he too has glimpsed the secrets of the sacred book of truth. He knows what to expect and is bursting with excitement. The day is coming — and coming soon — when all will be revealed. The Lord himself will return and pull back the curtain. The Lamb of God, with the marks of slaughter upon him (*cf* Rev. 5:6), will break the seals and open the book (*cf* Rev. 5:9). What John has seen in advance is only a glimpse of what is yet to be revealed. He tries to put it down in writing, but he is lost for words. Words alone cannot express the things he has seen and heard; and so he has to use signs and symbols that are not too clear at times to his readers or perhaps even to himself. Much mystery remains, but he has seen enough to convince him utterly that the triumph of Christ's kingdom is assured beyond a peradventure or a doubt. Unlike other seers before him, however, he is not to keep it secret. He is to blazon it abroad: 'Do not seal up the words of the prophecy of this book, for the time is near' (Rev. 22:10). He knows for a certainty what the outcome will be. Christ has died! Christ is risen! Christ will come again! To which he replies, 'Amen. Come, Lord Jesus!' (Rev. 22:20).

Nor is John alone in claiming to have received such a revelation. Paul too marvels at what he himself has seen and heard: 'I know a man in Christ who fourteen years ago was caught up to the third heaven ... and he heard things that cannot be told, which man may not utter' (II Cor. 12:2–4). But his assurance was not dependent simply on such an ecstatic experience or even on his life-changing experience on the Damascus road (*cf* Acts 9). It was an abiding certainty of faith which was his through a living relationship with his living Lord: 'What no eye has seen, nor ear heard, nor the heart of man conceived ... God has revealed to us through the Spirit' (I Cor. 2:9*f*). Nor was the revelation confined to 'the last things' and 'the time of the end'; it related to the temptations and trials of everyday life and gave him the confidence to live life triumphantly: 'I know whom I have believed, and I am sure that he is able to guard until that Day what has been entrusted to me' (II Tim. 1:12). He did not know all the answers; but he knew his Lord, and that left him in no doubt as to what the outcome would be.

Faith, for the Christian, is not, as for Alice in Wonderland, 'believing as many as six impossible things before breakfast'. It is 'the assurance of things hoped for, the conviction of things not seen' (Heb. 11:1). It is certain knowledge based on divine revelation. It is the human response to the divine disclosure. It is not simply something we exercise; it is something we receive. It is in fact a gift of God. We may not understand fully what we have seen and heard. But we have seen and heard enough to know that the final outcome is assured and that the powers of the kingdom will at last prevail. Then we shall understand fully, just as all along we have been fully understood (*cf* I Cor. 13:12).

2 Daniel's commission

Aware that he is to receive a divine revelation, Daniel prepares himself for its reception. As with the vision recorded in the previous chapter, he must not adopt a casual approach lest by so doing he dishonour God and fail to understand the vision. And so he goes into 'mourning for three weeks' (Dan. 10:2), showing signs of mortification befitting one who is about to engage in divine encounter. Prayer and fasting frequently accompany each other in the soul's search after God. Spiritual perception is closely related to physical condition and mental awareness.

Daniel is about to engage in a divine encounter and to receive a revelation which is 'out of this world'. The experience, he

E

knows, will be overwhelming, and this sense of fear and
foreboding is confirmed when he comes face to face with the
messenger of God who is to disclose to him what God himself
has planned. He is immediately struck by a sense of his
complete inadequacy and his utter unworthiness for the task
in hand. Like Moses (*cf* Ex. 4:10), and Jeremiah (*cf* Jer. 1:6),
he feels quite unworthy to receive God's word and, like Isaiah
(*cf* Isa. 6:5), he is altogether unprepared for such a revelation.

Daniel's reaction is perhaps not as common as it might be.
How can a man lightly take upon himself the role of witness
to the mysteries of God and messenger of the oracles of God?
Karl Barth had this question in mind when speaking of the
preacher who enters the pulpit with jaunty step, speaking
glibly, with an easy oratory, the unutterable oracles of God:

> 'What can it mean to preach? It means above all that we shall
> feel a fundamental alarm. What are you doing, young man, with
> the word of God upon *your* lips? Upon what grounds do you
> assume the role of mediator between heaven and earth? Who
> has authorised you to take your place there ... and, to crown
> all, to do so with results, with success? Did one ever hear of
> such overweening presumption, such brazenness? One does
> not with impunity usurp the perogatives of God! But does not
> the profession of the ministry inevitably involve both? ...
> Moses and Isaiah, Jeremiah and Jonah knew of a certainty why
> they did *not* want to enter into the preacher's situation ... Who
> dares, who can, preach, knowing what preaching is?'
> (*The Word of God and the Word of Man*, 1935, pp 125 *f*)

Those who have been called and commissioned by God to
make known the divine mysteries, be it through preaching or
in any other way, must do so. But they must do so with awe
and wonder, with sincerity and humility (*cf* Dan. 10:12), with
devotion and love as the mouthpiece of the living God.

Confronted, then, by the majestic angel, Daniel is completely
overawed: no strength is left in him, the colour drains from
his cheeks and he falls on his face to the ground (Dan. 10:8*f*).
It is for him a deeply personal experience, for 'the men who
were with [him] did not see the vision' (Dan. 10:7); nevertheless, the atmosphere is so charged by a sense of the otherness
of things that 'a great trembling fell upon them, and they fled

to hide themselves' (Dan. 10:7). Daniel shares in their trembling (Dan. 10:10); he is struck dumb (Dan. 10:15); and his breath leaves him (Dan. 10:17).

This account of the devastating effect of the apparition is so graphic that it suggests a similiar experience on the part of the writer himself. We are reminded in this connection of the call which came to Ezekiel (*cf* Ezek. 1:28; 3:26), or the experience of Saul on the Damascus road (*cf* Acts 9:8*f*). In this latter instance it is of interest to observe that, as in the case of Daniel, the men who were travelling with him were somehow aware that something unusual was happening: 'They stood speechless, hearing the voice but seeing no one' (Acts 9:7). So overwhelming, however, was the experience of Saul that he fell helplessly to the ground, blinded by the glory of such a revelation (*cf* Acts 9:8*f*). Less dramatically, but no less profoundly, the divine encounter has continued to effect and change the lives of countless people through the long centuries, not through an apparition, but through the living presence of the living Lord — timid souls have been transformed into courageous spirits, proud critics into humble worshippers and sinners into saints.

The effect of the vision on Daniel is devastating; but he is struck down only to be raised to his feet again, a better and a braver man. Three times over we read that the angel touched him. In the first instance it sets him on his feet: 'I fell on my face ... and behold, a hand touched me ... I stood up' (Dan. 10:9–11). At first the hand brings him trembling on to his 'hands and knees' (Dan. 10:10), crouching like a four-legged animal, afraid to look up; then it brings him to his feet, with the bearing and dignity of a man (Dan. 10:11). In the second instance the hand touches his lips (Dan. 10:16), as in the case of the prophet Isaiah (*cf* Isa. 6:7), restoring his speech and making it possible for him to commune with the divine messenger: 'then I opened my mouth and spoke' (Dan. 10:16). The divine encounter is able to restore a man's faculties and to give him gifts of thought, utterance and insight he has not possessed before: 'the blind receive their sight, the lame walk, lepers are cleansed, and the deaf hear' (Luke 7:22); 'he even ... makes the dumb speak' (Mark 7:37). In the third instance it gives him back his strength: '[he]

touched me and strengthened me' (Dan. 10:18). This, we are told, was the experience also of Jesus in the Garden of Gethsemane in his time of trial: 'and there appeared to him an angel from heaven, strengthening him' (Luke 22:43). Thank God for heavenly messengers, human and divine, who minister to God's people in their time of greatest need. And, of course, the words spoken by the angel to Daniel find an echo over and over again in Jesus' own words, as he touches this one and that: 'Fear not, peace be with you; be strong and of a good courage' (Dan: 10:19). Instead of fear he gives peace, for perfect love casts out fear (*cf* I John 4:18), and instead of trembling he gives strength to face whatever trials may come. 'Peace I leave with you; my peace I give to you ... Let not your hearts be troubled, neither let them be afraid' (John 4:27).

3   Angelic encounter

Much of Daniel's fear and trepidation is caused by a strange and wonderful apparition that appears before him as he 'was standing on the bank of the great river ... Tigris' (Dan. 10:4). It is the figure of 'a man clothed in linen' (Dan. 10:5), an un-named heavenly being who far outshines in glory and splendour even the archangels themselves, with belt of gold, body like beryl, face like lightning, eyes like flaming torches, arms and legs like burnished bronze and a voice like the noise of a multitude (Dan. 10:6). It is pointless to try and identify this glorious being, for the language is that of a theophany in which the divine majesty is revealed in all its splendour, light and power. It is an attempt to put into words what is ultimately indescribable. The writer attempts to do with words what the artist does with brush and paints — to capture in writing what he so deeply feels but cannot adequately express. Out of words are fashioned symbols and images which convey truth that lies beyond themselves. Of themselves they are inadequate; nevertheless, they are powerful vehicles of the reality they represent. To a man born blind, the colour scarlet can have little or no meaning, but when he is told it is 'like the sound of a trumpet', he 'sees' it in a new dimension and is able to grasp a meaning hitherto unknown.

The symbol not only represents, it also initiates; it gives an understanding, an appreciation, otherwis beyond our grasp. The language of religion is, to a considerable extent, the language of symbols. It takes us into regions of spiritual awareness that no purely descriptive prose can ever do. The figure described here by Daniel represents the unknown and the known, the hidden and the revealed, the visionary and the real in one.

It is hardly surprising that, despite the anonymity of the glorious 'man', early Christian commentators should have recognised in him a picture of the 'son of man' depicted in Revelation 1:13–16: '... with a golden girdle round his breast ... his eyes were like a flame of fire, his feet were like burnished bronze ... and his voice was like the sound of many waters'. This impression was no doubt strengthened by the sequel to this description: 'When I saw him, I fell at his feet as though dead. But he laid his right hand upon me, saying, "Fear not, I am the first and the last, and the living one; I died, and behold I am alive for evermore, and I have the keys of Death and Hades. Now write what you see, what is and what is to take place hereafter"' (Rev. 1:17–19). To the Christian believer the glorified Christ and the crucified Jesus are one, worthy of all worship, adoration and praise.

4 Angelic conflict

Following the account of Daniel's overwhelming vision the scene changes. There appears another heavenly being — perhaps to be identified with the archangel Gabriel — who reassures him and sets him on his feet again. As in 9:21 he has come as God's swift messenger in response to Daniel's prayer: 'your words have been heard, and I have come because of your words' (Dan. 10:12). It had been his intention to come at the beginning of Daniel's three week period of mourning with their fasting and prayer (*cf* Dan. 10:2), but for the full 'twenty-one days' (Dan. 10:13), he had been prevented from coming. But now, because Daniel had 'set [his] mind to understand and humbled [himself]' (Dan. 10:12), he had arrived and would 'make [him] understand what is to befall [his] people in the latter days' (Dan. 10:14).

The writer of the Book of Daniel takes prayer seriously. As soon as prayers are uttered with understanding and with humility they are heard in heaven itself and messengers are despatched to make known the mind and will of God. Both here and in the previous chapter, the divine response is immediate and direct. But sometimes, for reasons unknown to the one who prays, there is a delay in making that response known. What looks like 'unanswered prayer' may actually be 'delayed answer to prayer' caused by undisclosed factors which are nevertheless in the hands and in the control of God himself.

The reason for Gabriel's delay is a strange one: 'the prince of the kingdom of Persia withstood me twenty-one days' (Dan. 10:13). This is no earthly prince, but rather a heavenly counterpart, a symbolic angel-figure representing the king of Persia and his mighty empire which kept God's people captive. The picture behind this symbolic presentation may be that, common in antiquity, which thought of the nations, each with its own god whose responsibility it was to guard and protect that nation. In Isaiah 36:18*ff*, for example, the Assyrian commander asks: 'Has any of the gods of the nations delivered his land ...? Where are the gods of Hamath ... of Sepharvaim ... of Samaria? Who among all the gods of these countries have delivered their countries ... that the Lord should deliver Jerusalem?' That is, the nations of the world have their gods to look after their affairs; and Yahweh looks after his own people. There are suggestions elsewhere that these gods are in fact the 'sons of God', guardian angels (*cf* Deut. 32:8), set over the nations and forming a heavenly counterpart to the Gentile rulers into whose hands God, from time to time, has given his people. Thus, conflicts between nations here on earth mirror corresponding conflicts between their guardian angels in heaven; indeed, so closely are they related, that the heavenly conflict not only influences but even determines the conflict on earth. The guardian angel's triumph is reflected in the triumph of his nation, and conversely his defeat. They are powerful beings, as the kings and empires are whom they represent; but they exercise their authority, as the kings and empires do, only by permission of the sovereign Lord. As with the kings so also with their angelic princes, they will in the end be judged by God.

The princes who confront Gabriel in his divine mission are said to be the guardian angels of Persia and of Greece. 'The prince of the kingdom of Persia withstood me twenty-one days', but, says Gabriel, 'Michael, one of the chief princes, came to help me' (Dan. 10:13); '... I will return to fight against the prince of Persia; and when I am through with him, lo, the prince of Greece will come' (Dan. 10:20). Here, then, is the reason for Gabriel's delay. Meanwhile he can rely on Michael, the guardian angel of Israel, to 'hold the fort' till he returns!

This picture of heavenly princes and heavenly battles corresponding to earthly rulers and earthly wars is a strange, though graphic, symbol which is difficult to understand and to express in the thought-form of the present day. Indeed, the very attempt to do so robs it of its power of expression. Perhaps three comments may be tentatively made.

First, is that just as there is an evil in the world which is greater than the sum of individual sins, so there is a conflict which is greater than the conflicts we see going on around us. This is the reality that lies behind Paul's account of principalities and powers which cannot separate us from the love of God (*cf* Rom. 8:35*ff*). There is a 'corporate sense' which each generation receives from the one before and which it passes on to the one after; sometimes it is for the better and at other times for the worse, but always it is there, influencing contemporary event for good or for ill.

Second, is that 'nationhood' — like that of Persia, Greece or Israel — is more extensive and more profound than simply its contemporary expression. It is something which the words 'tradition', 'consciousness' and 'culture' hint at, but do not wholly define. Once more, it is something that each generation inherits and to which each generation contributes. J J Collins writes:

> 'The heavenly princes symbolise a surplus of power and meaning, over and above what is rationally controlled, whether it is for good or evil. The prince of Greece symbolises the whole impact of Hellenistic civilisation, far beyond what was consciously controlled by Antiochus Epiphanes. Michael, prince of Israel, represents a resource for the persecuted Jews, beyond what they could expect of themselves'.
>
> (*Daniel, I–II Maccabees, Old Testament Message* 16, 1981, p 101).

Third, is that 'heaven' is not indifferent to what takes place on earth. God hears the prayers of men and women and controls the affairs of nations. The sweep of history and the signs of the end are alike in his hands. His people need have no fear. Man proposes, but God disposes. He alone is King.

11

An Historical Drama

1   The stage: the world

At last we come to the vision itself which the angel showed to
Daniel: 'and now I will show you the truth' (Dan. 11:2). The
scene is set and the vision is described. It is in fact a brief
sketch of world history from Persian times down to the reign
of Antiochus, becoming somewhat more detailed as the
picture unfolds. The absence of name references gives a
sense of mystery and re-inforces the impression, conveyed by
the adoption of pseudonymity, that this panorama of people
and events is an actual forecasting of history from the time of
the Persian empire onwards. Taking his stand in the sixth
century, our second century author throws the past and the
present into the future in such a way that the past is seen as a
verifiable forecast of the future, and the present is seen as an
immediate prelude to 'the end'.

It is too facile a judgment to say that the phenomenon of
pseudonymity, so common in apocalyptic writings generally,
is 'a deception', contrived to hoodwink the readers into
imagining that, since 'the future' has been so accurately
predicted, then the prediction of the approaching 'end' can
be trusted also to come to pass. Rather, we are to see in it an
accepted literary device underlining the fact that God is the
Lord of history, that the whole sweep of history is under his
control and that the nations of the world and their rulers are
ultimately responsible to him and to him alone.

In a number of the apocalyptic books of this time the unity
and the universality of history, together with the accountability
of all rulers, are viewed in terms of great epochs into which
history is divided which are determined beforehand and
systematically arranged, all of them in the control of the God

of Israel. Despite their generally pessimistic view of history, the writers are essentially men of faith who are convinced that, even in the darkest days of persecution, God has not forsaken them; that, even though tyrants may for the time being be completely in control, the real authority still lies in the hands of God; and that, though great empires may seem altogether invincible, they will be superceded in God's good time.

Like Daniel, however, they come to such conclusions, not so much by looking into the past for evidence of God's deliverance or control, as by looking into the future for signs of the coming kingdom and his rule over all the nations of the earth. That future, they are convinced, is almost upon them. They believe themselves to be actors in the final act of a great cosmic drama which had its beginnings at the very dawn of creation and will reach its denouement in their own lifetime. Soon it will be enacted on their own world-stage and they themselves will be involved in it. Wrongs will at last be set right. The curtain will come down on history as they have known it, and God's Rule will begin.

This perception on the part of the apocalyptic writers is worth pondering — that the denouement holds the key to the play itself; that the wholeness of history can be seen in true perspective only when seen in the light of its consummation; that comprehension lies in completion; and that life is to be understood forwards and not just backwards. As part and parcel of the process of history, we ourselves are in no position to view it objectively or to pass final judgment upon it. Only at 'the end' can we see and understand 'the whole' in terms of the eternal purpose and infinite wisdom of God. From our vantage point on the stage of history, and as participants in the action itself, it is difficult for us to detect any pattern or plan either in history as such or in the narrow span of a single human life. But to the eye of faith, and from the vantage point of God's kingdom, the contours become clearer and we catch a glimpse of the intention and purpose of God.

The apocalyptic writers believe, as we have observed, that the whole course of human history, including 'the end', is predetermined by God. As Daniel says: 'what is determined shall be done' (Dan. 11:36). It has to be borne in mind, however, that although the course of historical events may be pre-determined, individuals such as the 'apostates' who sided with Antiochus and his Hellenizing ways can still be held respon-sible for their actions. The fact is that for these writers the clash between divine control and human freedom has not yet become a conscious problem. They are still able to say, with the writer of an early Jewish tractate, 'All is foreseen, but freedom of choice is given' (*Pirke Abot* 3:16). There is perhaps more truth in such a statement and in such an attitude of mind than the modern mind is willing to comprehend.

Herbert Butterfield illustrates this balance of divine control and human freedom by reference to the world of music. A musician plays over a piece of orchestral music for the first time, and in so doing is tempted to think of his own part as the leading one. But the fact is that the only thing he sees is the part to be played by his own instrument; and even that is limited, for he does not know what is coming on the next page. It is only when he and the other members of the orchestra play the work over together to the very end that he will see what the whole score is about. But even that analogy is not sufficiently flexible:

> 'We must imagine that the composer himself is only composing the music inch by inch as the orchestra is playing it, so that, if you and I play wrong notes, he changes his mind and gives a different turn to the bars that come immediately afterwards ... The composer leaves himself room for great elasticity until we ourselves have shown what we are going to do next; ... When the music has been played over and has become a thing of the past, we may be tempted to imagine ... that the whole course of things had been inevitable from the first.'
>
> (*Op cit* pp 94*ff*)

All is foreseen, but freedom of choice is given.

2 The actors: Gentile rulers and the Jews

The 'play' presented here is really a series of little cameos depicting the history of Gentile kings and kingdoms and God's own people Israel over the years right down to the time of writing — and beyond. The identification of the several characters need not concern us here in any detail. What is presented is the age-long story of intrigue and war, violence and suffering, conquest and suppression, hope and despair, treachery and persecution. It is surely a sad reflection on human nature — and on world politics — that the key words of these verses still retain their relevance today; words like riches, power, violence, flattery, deceit, favours, fear, arrogance and persecution. When we read these words and see them acted out before our eyes, we realise that the account given in this chapter does indeed concern our own time, reflecting as it does human passions and power politics as well as the hopes and fears of ordinary men and women.

No names are given as the chief actors troop on to the stage; but it is not too difficult to identify them as they take their bow one after another. Following four Persian kings 'three more kings ... and a fourth' (Dan. 11:2), come Alexander the Great ('a mighty king', Dan. 11:3*f*), then Ptolemy I ('the king of the south', Dan. 11:5), Berenice the daughter of Ptolemy II ('the daughter of the king of the south', Dan. 11:6), Antiochus II ('the king of the north', Dan. 11:6), Ptolemy III ('a branch', Dan. 11:7), Antiochus III ('the king of the north', Dan. 11:11,13), Heliodorus ('an exactor of tribute', Dan. 11:20), Antiochus IV ('a contemptible person', Dan. 11:21), the High Priest Onias III ('the prince of the covenant', Dan. 11:22), the Romans ('ships of Kittim', Dan. 11:30), the Jewish Hellenizers ('those who violate the covenant', Dan. 11:32) and the faithful Jews ('the people who know their God shall stand firm and take action', Dan. 11:32).

But this process of 'decoding' has led to quite different identifications by Jews and Christians alike down through the years. Medieval Jewish commentators, for example, saw in Daniel 11:36*ff* a reference to the emperor Constantine and, in the verses immediately preceding, an allusion to the destruction of the Temple by Titus in AD 70 (Dan. 11:31) and to the Bar Kochba Revolt in AD 132–5 (Dan. 11:34). Early Christian commentators, followed by many others throughout the succeeding centuries, detected in these same verses a reference to the Antichrist and related them to personalities and dramatic events of their own time.

This process has continued and in more modern times attempts have been made to interpret the Book of Daniel, and this chapter in particular, in terms of our own generation, identifying in its references such nations and organisations as the Soviet Union, Red China, the European Economic Community, NATO and the Warsaw Pact (see Introduction). As a result, the 'plain sense' of scripture is violated and analogy gives way to prediction of a purely subjective kind in which religious and political presuppositions readily provide the key to the code and determine the message conveyed. Such an approach to scripture is not only discredited in terms of scholarly pursuit, it is also unworthy in terms of religious quest. It is true that an audience, watching a play and observing the part played by this actor and that, may be able to see in it, and in them, reflections of their own experience and the events of their own time. Such analogy is legitimate and indeed helpful in understanding life as it now is. But this is altogether different from seeing in it and in its intention a foretelling of current events about which the author and the actors themselves have no inkling whatsoever.

3   The villain: Antiochus IV

The conflict described in this chapter finds its focus in the opposition to the Jewish people of the tyrant Antiochus who is presented here as chief actor and villain of the piece. He is introduced as 'a contemptible person' (Dan. 11:21) who, by flattery and force (Dan. 11:21*f*), by deceit and violence (Dan. 11:23*f*), by favour and falsehood (Dan. 11:26*f*), by seduction and self-glorification (Dan. 11:32,36) desecrates the holy sanctuary (Dan. 11:31) and persecutes the people of God (Dan. 11:33*ff*).

First, he attacks those who represent the covenant (Dan. 11:22), and 'takes action against the holy covenant' itself (Dan. 11:30). It was this covenant that made the Jews different from all the other people round about. This was the very basis of their religion and the reason for their distinctiveness. It was this that made them, in their own eyes and in the eyes of their neighbours, non-conformists and so dissidents and would-be rebels against authority. Such an attitude under such a totalitarian rule was quite unacceptable to the powers-that-be, as indeed it always is. Dissidents, by their very nature, are a threat to the solidarity of the state. They must conform or else give up their rights as citizens. To be different is to be dangerous. Jewish identity and Christian conviction single such people out as 'people of the covenant' more markedly than most other groups in the community, and as such they will continue to be regarded with suspicion and dis-ease by 'the world' as well as by 'the tyrant'.

Second, he divides and rules. He takes advantage of the growing division within the Jewish community and drives home his wedge: 'he shall seduce with flattery those who violate the covenant; but the people who know their God shall stand firm and take action' (Dan. 11:32). On the one hand, there were the so-called Hellenizers who were keen to support Antiochus's policy of Hellenization, despite the moral and religious dangers associated with it. For the most part they belonged to the wealthy, aristocratic, priestly families in Jerusalem with strong conservative tendencies and had much to gain from currying favour with the king. On the other hand, there were those, such as the Hasidim (as they came to be called), who were strongly opposed to such encroachments on their religion, who gave themselves to a study of the Law and who were prepared, if need be, to die rather than betray the law of their fathers. Such dissension in their ranks of the Jews — later to appear in the parties of the Sadducees and the Pharisees — was a godsend to Antiochus who encouraged it to suit his own purpose.

This same policy of divide and rule has been commonplace in every age in both politics and religion on the part of those who are determined to gain or maintain control. In our own day it continues to be used against the Christian Church in regimes which are suspicious or afraid of that Church's voice lest it undermine the authority of the state. Christian unity is of importance for many reasons and not least because a united Church can more readily speak with one voice and more effectively carry out its mission to the world.

Third, he denigrates their religion and desecrates their Temple: his 'forces ... appear and profane the temple ... and take away the continual burnt offering and ... set up the abomination that makes desolate' (Dan. 11:31). In December, 168 BC, Antiochus's soldiers attacked and desecrated the Temple where, for three years, the worship of God was forbidden. On top of the sacred altar an image of the Greek god Zeus was set up and swine's flesh sacrificed on it. This abomination remained until the cleansing of the Temple by Judas Maccabeus three years later. Besides all this, the rite of circumcision was proscribed, as was the observance of the Sabbath and the recognised feast days. Books of the Law were defaced or destroyed, and Jews were forced to eat swine's flesh and sacrifice to foreign gods (*cf* I Macc. 1:41*ff*). Refusal to comply carried with it the penalty of death. Many suffered much cruelty and others were slain.

More suffering has been caused in the name of religion or in defence of religion than perhaps by any other single factor. The reasons for religious persecution are many; but the venom with which it is often perpetrated is difficult to understand. Simple people with a simple faith are suddenly seen as a menace to the state or the *status quo*. The charges sometimes levelled against them are 'defamation of the state' or 'breach of the civil law', and the severity of the penalties passed is often quite out of proportion to the crime committed. Religious liberty is a fundamental freedom which must be protected against all encroachment. An attack on such freedom is an attack on God himself.

That perhaps is why, in the *fourth* place, Antiochus demands from the Jews an allegiance which only God can require: he begins to 'exalt himself and magnify himself above every god, and [to] speak astonishing things against the God of gods' (Dan. 11:36). So exalted does he become in his own estimation that he renounces 'the gods of his fathers' and the fertility god Tammuz, 'the one beloved by women' (Dan. 11:37), the consort of Ishtar the goddess of love. Instead he honours 'the god of fortresses' (Dan. 11:38), Zeus himself, whose image he sets up in the Temple, with features resembling his own! He calls himself Epiphanes, 'God Manifest', and in the most holy sanctuary virtually takes the place of God.

The glamorous god Tammuz is still popular — and not only among women. So too is Zeus, the god of fortresses, who relies on weapons of war to propagate his beliefs. But the crowning infamy is to set oneself up in the place of God, and this men do whenever they deny his right to reign. To deny God and to set onself up in his place is to deny the very ground of one's being and to commit the ultimate sin of blasphemy. Antiochus is not alone in this; nor are the leaders and rulers of the nations. The role of the villain is an attractive one which we would all aspire to play — if only in our dreams.

4   The heroes: 'the wise'

In contrast to the villain Antiochus, the 'heroes' now file on to the stage — like martyrs entering the arena to be mauled by the wild beasts. They are the 'maskilim' — 'the people who are wise [who] shall make many understand, though they shall fall by sword and flame' (Dan. 11:33). It has been generally assumed that these 'maskilim' or 'wise ones' are to be identified with the Hasidim or 'pious ones' to whom three references are made in the Books of Maccabees (*cf* I Macc. 2:42, 7:12*f*; II Macc. 14:6), who are described as 'mighty warriors of Israel' (I Macc. 2:42) and who may be thought of as forerunners of the Pharisees and the Essenes. Such identification, however, is open to question; but the 'maskilim' had this at least in common with the Hasidim, they represented a form of pietism dedicated to the worship and service of God in face of great opposition. It was no doubt from this milieu that the Book of Daniel itself came.

From the stories recorded in chapters 1–6 we learn that they were men of prayer, passionately opposed to idolatry, strict in their observance of Jewish law and endowed with divine wisdom. From the visions in chapters 7–12 we learn, not only that they were men of prayer who repented for the sins of their people, but also that they were teachers who diligently taught 'the many' the Law of God and the meaning of that secret tradition which they themselves had received in visions and dreams and through the medium of angels. They were highly critical of their Gentile rulers who not only persecuted the faithful, but above all challenged God himself. They were not, however, particularly concerned about political involvement, and military intervention they apparently regarded as only 'a little help' (Dan. 11:34). They were ready to lay down their lives for the sake of their religion, as indeed many of them did (*cf* Dan. 11:33*f*). It is true that they seemed to envisage an earthly kingdom; but they were more concerned about the purification of themselves and those they taught (*cf* Dan. 11:35). They believed, moreover, that above and beyond this physical and material world was a world of spiritual power and that these two were closely related. Salvation would come, not by military might or by earthly power, but by divine deliverance. Their hope was set in God alone, even though this might mean suffering and martyrdom for them and for 'the many'. Their expressed fears and implied warnings, however, fell on deaf ears, for soon came the Maccabean Revolt which, though it brought freedom from the tyranny of Antiochus, brought also much misery and destruction in its train.

The writer of Daniel sees in the martyrdom of 'the wise' an act of propitiation on behalf of 'the many', 'to refine and to cleanse them and to make them white' (Dan. 11:35). We are reminded here of the Suffering Servant of Isaiah who, through suffering and death, was able to 'make many to be accounted righteous and ... bear their iniquities' (Isa. 53:11). And this is how from the beginning the Christian Church viewed the suffering and death of Jesus which the world might regard as sheer folly but which is in fact 'the power of God and the wisdom of God' (I Cor. 1:24). At 'the time of the end' (Dan. 11:35), it too will be seen for what it is, for 'it is yet for the time appointed' (Dan. 11:35).

Godly wisdom is altogether different from that worldly wisdom which claims to be able to read the 'signs of the times' in terms of social trend or political movement or financial crisis. It is rather that godly discernment born out of a deep spirituality, which is open to the revelation of God and is able to look beyond the seen to the unseen and to interpret the temporal in terms of the eternal and of Jesus Christ who has been made 'our wisdom, our righteousness and sanctification and redemption' (I Cor. 1:30). Through his teaching we are made wise, and through his death we are purified and cleansed and presented 'without blemish before the presence of [God's] glory' (Jude 24).

12

The Final Act

1 Free at last

As the curtain goes up and the final act begins, Michael the archangel takes his place on centre stage, the champion and advocate of his people (Dan. 12:1). He has confronted the 'princes' of Persia and of Greece and has overcome them. He now stands before his people, their defender and deliverer. He has no 'speaking part' here, but his very presence is eloquent enough. That time has now arrived (Dan. 12:1), the time of God's appointing, the time for which all history has waited, the time of judgment, the Day of the Lord. His people are now to be vindicated once and for all and at last set free from bondage. Like the 'son of man' in chapter 7, he is to receive the dominion in which his people too will share.

But first: 'there shall be a time of trouble, such as never has been since there was a nation till that time' (Dan. 12:1). This is a recurring theme in subsequent apocalyptic books. In the Book of Jubilees, for example, we read concerning the end time: 'For calamity follows on calamity, and wound on wound, and tribulation on tribulation, and evil tidings on evil tidings ... All these will come on an evil generation' (Jub. 23:13*ff*). Elsewhere such troubles are referred to as 'the travail pains' of the Messiah or of the messianic kingdom. As pain is part of human birth, so it is also of the birth of the new age. Among the Hymns of Thanksgiving from Qumran, for example, we read of the emergence of God's redeemed people in these words:

> 'I am in distress
> like a woman in travail with her firstborn,
> when her pangs come

130

and grievous pain on her birth-stool,
causing torture in the crucible (*ie* womb) of the
pregnant one.'

(Hymns III 7*ff*).

Similarly in the New Testament the coming 'woes' are described in Mark 13:8 as 'the beginnings of the birth pangs' (*cf* Matt. 24:8), and in Revelations 12:2 the birth of the messianic community is likened, as at Qumran, to a woman who 'crieth out, travailing in birth, and in pain to be delivered'. The theme of 'salvation through suffering' is a constantly recurring one throughout the whole of the New Testament and finds its focus in the person and work of Jesus the Messiah who 'through what he suffered ... became the source of eternal salvation to all who obey him' (Heb. 5:8*f*). Wherever the Messiah appears or the powers of the kingdom are made evident — at the time of the end or in the hurly-burly of our modern world — there we may expect the powers of darkness to assemble to do battle against the people of God.

The message of this chapter is that, whatever the pain and whatever the tribulation, deliverance belongs to God: 'your people shall be delivered' (Dan. 12:1). It is as old as the exodus itself; but here the writer goes further than any other writer in the Old Testament. The deliverance that God will bring about will not be simply deliverance of the nation from the hands of Antiochus the tyrant, but deliverance of men and women from the power of death itself. Many of the surrounding nations celebrated victory over death in their liturgies as they enacted and re-enacted, in their myths and rituals, the demise of mother-nature in the icy grip of winter and its rising again to new life with the return of every spring. And what the heathen witnessed in nature and in the cycles of the seasons, that the Hebrew prophets saw in the history of their own nation and in the rise and fall of empires. In the captivities of Egypt under Pharaoh and of Babylon under Nebuchadnezzar they had encountered a living death: Egypt was indeed a fiery furnace, and Babylon a lions' den. But in each place they had been rescued by the living God who had preserved them from the flames and had shut the lions' mouths, and he would do so again. This was the faith so graphically portrayed by the prophet Ezekiel who likened his people to a valley full of bones: God would breathe into them and they would stand up and live, an exceeding great host. He would raise up his people from their graves and bring them back to the land of their fathers (*cf* Ezek. 37:1–14).

But here in Daniel we have a hope expressed that goes far beyond any to be found in Ezekiel. The deliverance envisaged is not a figurative resurrection of the nation, but an actual resurrection of the faithful few. These are described as 'the wise' or 'those who understand' who will be vindicated in the end and will be raised by God to share in the coming kingdom. No doubt the author has in mind here the struggle in his own day between those Jews who remained faithful to the Torah and the 'apostates' who sided with Antiochus and his Hellenising ways and in particular those who had suffered for the stand they had taken. These 'wise', among whom the martyrs have an honoured place, will be delivered even from death itself and will rise in glorious resurrection. Hints are given elsewhere in the Old Testament of life after death, but here in Daniel we have the first unambiguous reference to the life beyond in terms of resurrection (*cf* Isa. 26:19, which may refer to the resurrection of the nation as in Ezek. 37). For this reason this chapter holds an unique place in the scriptural revelation.

It would be wrong, however, to try and find in these verses anything like a doctrine of the last things. There is much here that is enigmatic and tentative and obscure. The writer is expressing a deeply-felt conviction, borne in upon him no doubt by the happenings of his own day and in particular by the martyrdom of those among 'the wise' and 'the righteous' in Israel. The form in which his conviction takes shape is that of resurrection. But the precise nature of that resurrection is left to later writers to expound, to speculate upon and to develop. This was done not only by subsequent apocalyptic writers, but also within the circle of the Pharisees and of course within the Christian Church itself. Limited though its understanding is, the Book of Daniel marks here a great advance in spiritual insight. Gone is the old notion of Sheol and its shades as the final abode of all mankind. A light has shone into the darkness, however dimly, which will eventually grow into the brilliance of Easter Day. Michael may stand silently on centre stage; but the sound of music fills the air as prophets, saints and martyrs take up the strain and cry as with one voice, 'Free at last!'

'Death is swallowed up in victory. O death, where is thy victory? O death, where is thy sting? ... Thanks be to God who gives us the victory through our Lord Jesus Christ' (I Cor. 15:54 *ff*). Deliverance indeed!

2 The future hope

When we examine possible reasons for the development at this time of the belief in life after death in the form of resurrection we have to bear in mind at least two things. One is, as already indicated, the prevailing circumstances when many faithful Israelites were martyred for their religion. The other is that reflective piety which marked the life of many and which asked with increasing urgency certain basic questions about both life and death.

How was it possible that that precious communion which righteous men had enjoyed with God should suddenly and irrevocably be brought to an end by the cruel blow of death, especially if it had been struck by an enemy of the Jewish religion? There must surely be the possibility of its continuation and fulfilment in conditions other than those of Sheol where 'the dead do not praise the Lord, nor do any that go down into silence' (Ps. 115:17), where all things come alike to all and where there is 'one fate ... to the righteous and the wicked' (Eccles. 9:2). The same questions had been asked by the Psalmists. But now they were being asked with a new urgency in the light of the events of the author's day.

Then there was the question of theodicy: how was it possible to vindicate a righteous God in face of the blatant injustices perpetrated against his faithful worshippers? This had greatly troubled the writers of Job and Ecclesiastes who attempted answers which carried less than conviction and brought little comfort to men like the author of Daniel who faced the inexplicable tragedies of his day. If justice must be seen to be done — and God is just — then it must find its confirmation beyond the final boundary of human experience, death itself. He does not see clearly wherein this vindication lies or what form it will take. What really matters to him is the assertion itself that God is just and must be vindicated in the end.

Bound up with this was the question of God's purpose in history and indeed in creation itself. Is that purpose really fulfilled in the course of history as it unfolds and in the working out of the natural order? Or does the answer lie in some life and in some order beyond this one, a transcendent order of being and a transcendent order of creation in which human life and all created things will realise their potential and reveal the glory that God intended should be theirs from the beginning?

If this is so, what form should man's survival take in the life beyond death? To the author of Daniel such survival could not be simply the 'natural' continuation of what the Greeks called 'the psyche' or 'the soul'. A doctrine of 'natural immortality' would not do justice either to God as 'the living God' or to man as 'a living personality'. Only a belief in resurrection could overcome these difficulties; for in resurrection God is seen to be actively at work, taking the initiative and demonstrating his power to justify and save; and in resurrection man, in the totality of his being and not just as a 'truncated soul', receives God's blessing and enters into the promise of God's reward.

The author of Daniel may not have been consciously aware of such specific questions just as he was not clearly aware of the specific nature of resurrection itself. His understanding of such things was limited (*cf* Dan. 12:8). But he believed that such understanding as he had belonged to the mysteries of God and had been revealed to him as disclosures of eternal truth.

3   The resurrection

The deliverance, then, that is promised is not just that of the nation as such, but of 'every one whose name shall be found written in the book' (Dan. 12:1). This is 'the book of remembrance' (Mal. 3:16), or 'the book of life' (Isa. 4:3; Rev. 3:5, *etc*) to which reference is made elsewhere in scripture. These favoured ones are identified in a later verse as 'those who are wise' and as 'those that shall make many understand' (Dan. 12:3; *cf* Dan. 11:33); like the Suffering Servant in Isaiah they 'make many to be accounted righteous' and 'bear their iniquities' (Isa. 53:11).

It is they who are counted among the 'many of those who sleep in the dust of the earth [who] shall awake' in resurrection (Dan. 12:2). This resurrection is not for all; nor is it only for the righteous. It is for the pre-eminently good and the pre-eminently bad, the martyrs and their murderers. The one will rise to 'everlasting life' and the other to 'shame and everlasting contempt' (Dan. 12:2). In this way God is vindicated not only in the reward of the righteous, but also in the punishment of the wicked. Moral distinctions are thus continued into the life beyond death as are the consequences of human endeavour. This is something quite different from either the immortality of the Greeks or the shadowy existence of Sheol. Special rewards and punishments are reserved for the special few. Nothing more is said about the fate of 'the wicked' or of 'the wise' except that the latter 'shall shine like the brightness of the firmament' and will be 'like the stars for ever and ever' (Dan. 12:3), *ie* in the coming kingdom (on earth?) they will be given a place of glory and honour, or perhaps in heaven itself they will share the glory and splendour that belongs to the angels.

The author's attention, then, is focussed on 'the wise' and in particular on the martyrs who have laid down their lives for their religion. Out of focus, and indeed out of sight, are such questions as the fate of 'the wicked' who remain unpunished and the state of 'the many' righteous who remain unrewarded, the nature of the resurrection itself and the bodies in which the dead will be raised, the relationship between the course of history and what lies beyond 'the end'.

The Christian Church, then, was born into a Jewish world in which belief in the resurrection was already well established. Many queries still continued and many mysteries remained: In what form will the resurrected dead appear? What will be the fate of the wicked? When will the judgment take place and what form will it assume? What will happen to those who are still alive at 'the last time'? What will be the sequence of events when 'the last trump' sounds? Many such questions had been asked before by Jewish teachers and would continue to be asked. But there was one fundamental difference between the teaching of, say, Daniel, and the teaching of, say, Paul. It lay in the resurrection of Jesus Christ from the dead. The authority by which Daniel wrote was the word of an angel; the authority by which the Church spoke was the event that took place that first Easter morning and the presence with them thereafter of their living Lord. The Christians shared with the Jews the glorious hope of resurrection, but theirs was 'a living hope through the [actual] resurrection of Jesus Christ from the dead' (I Peter 1:3). His resurrection was completely central to their faith — and still is. Not only did it vindicate their belief in an all-loving and all-powerful God, it confirmed their faith in Jesus as the Son of God and was at the same time the guarantee of their own resurrection, for by his resurrection Jesus had become 'the first fruits of those who have fallen asleep' (I Cor. 15:20). So fundamental was his resurrection for Paul that he could write to the Corinthian Church: 'If Christ has not been raised, your faith is futile and you are still in your sins. Then those also who have fallen asleep in Christ have perished' (I Cor. 15:17*f*). It may be true that no 'empirical proof' is possible and that by its very nature the resurrection of Jesus lies beyond the reach of 'objective evidence'. But this is not to deny its objective reality. It rests solidly on the faith of the Church which in turn rests squarely on the Gospel record: the empty tomb, the birth and continuing witness of the Church and the experience of all who know him as the living Lord.

4   An epilogue

The vision is over. The angel gives Daniel instructions on what he must now do (*cf* Dan. 12:4), and Daniel responds by asking the same question he had asked on a previous occasion: 'How long ... till the end?' (Dan. 12:6). Much of what is said here is a repetition of what has gone before. But we may note in these verses and in the final two chapters as a whole four things of lasting worth.

First, those who have received God's revelation are eventually to make it known. Daniel is among the wise who understand what none of the wicked understood (Dan. 12:10). He has been introduced to the mysteries of God and is told to 'seal the book' (Dan. 12:4) in which these mysteries are recorded and to preserve them 'until the time of the end' (Dan. 12:4). That time has now arrived and so he has to make them known. The wise must not keep their newly found wisdom to themselves; it is their responsibility, as it were, to break the seal and to 'make many understand' (Dan. 11:33), disclosing to them things they could never have discovered for themselves.

The disciples of Jesus likewise receive from their Master the secrets of the kingdom of heaven (Mark 4:1), and are numbered among the truly wise (*cf* I Cor. 1:30). But unlike Daniel they have no need to seal up their message until some future 'end time', for with Jesus that 'end' has already come and with his resurrection and the gift of the Spirit that kingdom has come 'with power' (*cf* Mark 9:1; Rom. 1:4). Having 'presented himself alive [to them] after his passion by many proofs' (Acts 1:3), he bids them to be his witnesses 'in Jerusalem and in all Judea and Samaria and to the end of the earth' (Acts 1:8). His great commission then is the continuing commission he still gives to his Church: 'Go therefore and make disciples of all nations, baptizing them in the name of the Father and of the Son and of the Holy Spirit, teaching them to observe all that I have commanded you; and lo, I am with you always, to the close of the age' (Matt. 28:19*f*).

Second, there will be a time of trouble, but it will come to an end: 'The wicked shall do wickedly ... the continual burnt offering is taken away, and the abomination that makes desolate is set up' (Dan. 12:10*f*). But the time of deliverance is near (Dan. 12:7*ff*). The time of trouble, however, is more in evidence than the time of the end, and the chaos caused by wicked rulers is more obvious than indications of divine providence. There is an element of contingency and of chance which makes the course of history quite unpredictable; the incidence of moral evil challenges faith in an all-gracious, all-powerful God; and the fact of man's vaunted freedom to do evil as well as good does much to deny that God is in control. In the light of all this the question is often raised as to whether we can really detect any divine plan in history at all which declares that all is well with the world.

It has to be remembered, however, that belief in the divine control of history is 'not based on an intricate calculus, resulting in a sort of profit and loss trading account, to show that on the whole there is more good than evil in the world' (H W Robinson, *The Veil of God*, 1936, p 27). For the Christian it is based rather on God's revelation of himself in his Son our Lord whose death and resurrection give a new interpretation and meaning to history. Behind and beyond this 'natural world' with its ebb and flow of evil and of good, there lies a 'spiritual world' which gives meaning and purpose to the whole. The course of history is to be judged, moreover, in terms of 'the end', and its meaning is to be understood in terms of the eternal God. The writer of Daniel catches a glimpse of this revealed mystery and, through his book, has placed mankind eternally in his debt.

Third, the time of the end is in God's hands, not ours. 'How long shall it be' asks Daniel, 'till the end of these wonders?' (Dan. 12:6). Already, in an earlier chapter, the interval is given as 'a time, two times, and half a time' (Dan. 7:25). Elsewhere it is 'two thousand and three hundred evenings and mornings' (Dan. 8:14), *ie* 1150 days. Now two more numbers are added: 'one thousand two hundred and ninety days' (Dan. 12:11) and 'one thousand three hundred and thirty-five days' (Dan. 12:12). It may be that these later figures are attempted 'corrections' of the one in Daniel 8:14 or else they may refer to different events associated with 'the end'. Whatever the explanation may be, the impression is left that men will always remain confused about matters which God alone can disclose. As Jesus said to his enquiring disciples, 'It is not for you to know times and seasons which the Father has fixed by his own authority. But you shall receive power when the Holy Spirit has come upon you; and you shall be my witnesses' (Acts 1:7*f*). This should be sufficient warning to all those who, with subtle prognostication and with the help of charts and calculations, try to work out the exact time of 'the end'. That 'end' is in God's keeping and the time of its coming is for him alone to disclose.

And *fourth*, we can rest in the assurance of God's promised word: 'Go your way till the end; and you shall rest, and shall stand in your allotted place at the end of the days' (Dan. 12:13). Daniel is not to worry. The future and the consummation are in God's control and he will bring it to pass. A place has been prepared for him (*cf* John 14:2) and he will be at rest in God's eternal kingdom. These words clearly recall the words of Jesus to his disciples: 'Peace I leave with you; my peace I give to you; not as the world gives do I give to you. Let not your hearts be troubled, neither let them be afraid' (John 14:27). The Christian hope is based, not on a heavenly vision and not on the word of an angel, but on the word of Christ himself who was 'crucified, dead and buried' and who, on the third day, rose again from the dead. It is a hope that sustains in life — and in death.

This hope was graphically demonstrated in the case of a young student preparing for the Christian ministry at Glasgow University in the dark days of the Second World War. Returning home in the early hours of the morning from fire-watching duty and after a devastating night of enemy bombing, he found his home a heap of smouldering rubble. Clambering on top of it he clawed in desperation till his fingers bled in a vain attempt to rescue his parents and other members of the family who were buried underneath. And as he stood there, utterly helpless and distraught, a piece of notepaper came fluttering out of the ruins and settled at his feet. Picking it up, he recognised it at once and in that moment found God's assurance in his time of desperate need, for it was a page out of one of his own sermons — on the resurrection of Jesus Christ from the dead.

Christ has died, Christ is risen, Christ will come again,
Hallelujah.

Further Reading

Anderson, R A, *Signs and Wonders*, International Theological Commentary, (Eerdmans and Handsel Press, 1984)

Baldwin, J G, *Daniel: an introduction and commentary*, (Inter Varsity Press, 1978)

Barr, J, *Daniel*, Peake's Commentary, (Nelson, revd. 1962)

Collins, J J, *Daniel, I–II Maccabees*, Old Testament Message 16, (Michael Glazier, 1981)

Hartman, L F and Di Lella, A A, *The Book of Daniel*, Anchor Bible, (Doubleday, 1977)

Heaton, E W, *The Book of Daniel*, Torch Bible Commentary, (SCM, 1956)

Jeffery, A and Kennedy, G, *The Book of Daniel*, The Interpreter's Bible, vol 6, (Abingdon, 1956)

Lacoque, A, *The Book of Daniel*, translated by D Pellauer, (John Knox Press, 1979)

Lüthi, W, *The Church to Come*, (Hodder and Stoughton, 1939)

Montgomery, J A, *The Book of Daniel*, International Critical Commentary, (T and T Clark, 1927)

Porteous, N W, *Daniel*, Old Testament Library, (SCM and Westminster Press, 1979)

Russell, D S, *Daniel*, The Daily Study Bible, (The Saint Andrew Press, 1981)

Towner, W S, *Daniel*, Interpretation, (John Knox, 1984)